Henry Onderdonk

Jamaica Centennial

July 4th, 1876

Henry Onderdonk

Jamaica Centennial
July 4th, 1876

ISBN/EAN: 9783743414648

Manufactured in Europe, USA, Canada, Australia, Japa

Cover: Foto ©ninafisch / pixelio.de

Manufactured and distributed by brebook publishing software (www.brebook.com)

Henry Onderdonk

Jamaica Centennial

the Presbyterian Church.

JAMAICA CENTENNIAL,

JULY 4th, 1876.

ALSO,

RECOLLECTIONS

OF

SCHOOL AND COLLEGE LIFE.

BY

HENRY ONDERDONK, Jr.

JAMAICA, L. I.

1876.

The committee appointed to make arrangements for the approaching celebration of the Fourth of July met, pursuant to adjournment, as a Committee of the Whole in the Town Hall on Friday evening last, and after due consideration the following resolutions were passed.

Resolved, That HENRY ONDERDONK, Jr. Esq. be invited to read a historical paper upon events that occurred in and near the vicinity of Jamaica, during the Revolution.

Also, That Hon. RICHARD BUSTEED and Rev. J. G. Van Slyke be requested to deliver orations.

Also, That W. J. BALLARD be requested to select one of the young ladies of the Public School to read the Declaration of Independence, and to make arrangements for singing by the pupils of the Public School.

Also, That these exercises be held in the Town Hall, July 4th, 1876, commencing at 10 o'clock, A. M. and ending at 12 M., precisely, when the audience will join in singing the Doxology.

Also, That the citizens be requested to decorate their houses during the day with flags, &c. and illuminate them during the evening.

Also, Upon motion Mr. C. H. HUNTING was appointed a committee to make arrangements for firing one hundred guns during the day.

And upon motion Messrs T. F. ANCHEN, JOHN FLEURY and B. F. EVERETT were appointed to make arrangements for a parade of the Fire Department in the evening.

Adjourned to meet at the Town Hall on Wednesday evening, June 14th at 8 o'clock.

A. A. DEGRAUW, *Chairman.*
W. J. BALLARD, *Secretary.*

OLDEN TIMES.

An Additonal Installment of Henry Onderdonk's Unspoken Address on the Revolutionary History of Jamaica.

"No Taxation Without Representation"—The Men Who Voted in 1775—The Jamaica Militia and the Pay Roll in 1776—Some Very Interesting Facts.

In printing Mr. Onderdonk's sketches of Revolutionary Incidents at Jamaica, we omitted the introductory portion which shows how the patriots gradually drifted into open rebellion after their petitions had been spurned from the foot of the throne.

VIEWS OF OUR FOREFATHERS.

When our forefathers first entered on the Revolutionary struggle, they did not contemplate a separation from the British Crown; but merely desired the reform of abuses and to resist the encroachments of Parliament and the Ministry on their rights and privileges. Their *motto* was "No taxation without Representation." But they advanced on step by step, till at last there could be no return, and then, they went into open rebellion. No doubt some long headed statesmen saw from the first that this would be the final result.

FIRST MOVEMENT IN JAMAICA.

On the passage of the Bill in Parliament, shutting up the port of Boston for throwing tea overboard, some persons in Jamaica assembled at the inn of Increase Carpenter, 2 miles east of the village, and after an interchange of opinions requested Othniel Smith, the constable, to warn the freeholders to a meeting at the Court House (where now is the Hall of Pharmacy), to take into consideration the state of public affairs.

RESOLUTIONS ADOPTED.

The inhabitants of Jamaica met Dec. 6th, 1774, and resolved:

1, To maintain the just dependence of the Colonies upon the Crown of Great Britain, and to render true allegiance to King George III.
2. That it is our right to be taxed only by our own consent; and that taxes imposed on us by Parliament are an infringement of our rights.
3. We glory to have been born subject to the Crown and excellent Constitution of Great Britain; we are one people with our mother country, and lament the late unhappy disputes.
5. We sympathize with our brethren of Boston under their sufferings.
6. We approve the measures of the late General Congress at Philadelphia.
7. We appoint for our Committee of correspondence and observation:

Rev. Abm. Keteltas,	Capt. Richard Betts,
Waters Smith,	Dr. John Innes,
Capt. Ephraim Bailey,	Jos. Robinson,
Capt. Jos. French,	Elias Bailey,
Wm. Ludlum.	

NOTE.—This meeting would have been held much sooner but for the refusal of Capt. Benj. Whitehead Supervisor to show the townspeople the letter he had received from the Whig Committee of New York.

NOTE.—Abm. Keteltas tho' a clergyman said that sooner than pay the duty on tea as required by Parliament he would shoulder his musket and fight.

TRUE PREDICTION OF THE COMMITTEE.

The Jamaica Committee met Jan. 19th, 1775, and after thanking the New York delegates to the General Congress for their important services, they say: "We joyfully anticipate the pleasure of seeing your names enrolled in the annals of America and transmitted to the latest generations as the friends and deliverers of your country, and of having your praises resounded from one end of this Continent to the other."

PROTEST OF THE LOYALISTS.

Only 8 days after the Committee had thus endorsed the action of their delegates, 136 inhabitants of Jamaica signed a protest stating that "a few people of the town had taken on themselves the name of a Committee. We never gave our assent thereto, as we disapprove of all unlawful meetings. We resolve to continue faithful subjects to His Majesty King George III our most gracious Sovereign."

THE FIRST POLL LIST.

1775, Mar. 31st.—Friday being the day appointed for taking the sense of the freeholders of Jamaica on the expediency of choosing a deputy to the Provincial Congress at New York, a poll was opened at the Court House. The town refused by a majority of nine to send a deputy.

NO COMMITTEE—NO DEPUTY.

Adam Lawrence,
Johannes Polhemus,
Jos. Oldfield,
Tunis Bargin,
Chas. Arding,
John Lamoerson,
John Smith,
John Troup,
Paul Amberman,
Johannes Lott,
Johannes Snedeker,
Jos. Golder,
Abm. Ditmars,
Jacamiah Valentine,
Wm. Cornell,
Isaac Amberman,
Lucas Elderd,
St. Lott,
Wm. Welling,
Nich. Van Osdoll,
Lucas Bergen,
John Wiggins,
Oba. Mills,
Aury Ramson,
John Williamson,
Cor's Bennet,
Nich. Jones,
Samuel Doughty,
Daniel Ramson,
John Foster,
Thomas Betts,
John Bennet,
John Doughty,
Nathaniel Higbie,
Rich. Betts, Capt.
Tunis Covert,
Nich. Lamberson,
Simeon Lamberson,
Wm. Pettit,
Johanus Williamson,
Oba. Hinchman,
Jacob Bargin,
Nich. Ludlam,
Bernardus Ryder,
Phillip Platt,
Nath'l Mills, Jr.
Johannis Eldert,
Peter Noostrant,
Garret Noostrant,
Garret Dorland, Jr.,
Garret Dorland, Sr.,
Jacob Lott,
Nath'l Townsend,
Garret Snedeker,
Derrick Bargin,
St. Clements,
Abm. Van Nostrant,
Nath'l Mills, Jr.,
Matthias Lamberson,
George Ryerson,
John Ramson,
St. Higby,
John Ramson, Sr.,
Daniel Lawrence,
Geo. Dunbar,
Henry Higby,
Benj. Doughty,
Wm. Watts,
Wm. Golder,
Tho. Cornell,
John Van Liew,
Jabes Woodruff,
John Rowland,
Hope Mills,
Benj. Whitehead,
Nehemiah Carpenter,
Hendrick Emmeus,
Rem Ramson,
John Bargin,
Dowe Ditmis,
Evert Van Wickley,
Wm. Thatford,
Anthony Ramson,
John Nostrand,
Garret Latting,
Ludlam Smith,
Samuel Foster,
Isaac Letfert,
Rueloff Dur en,
Johannis Polhemus,
Jos. French, Esq.,
A. V. Nostrand,
John Watts,
Jost Van Brunt—94.

FOR A DEPUTY—JOS. ROBINSON.

Capt. Anthony Rutgers, Samuel Messenger,
John Skidmore, John J. Skidmore,
Robert Hinckman, Jaques Johnson,
Waters Smith, Neh. Everitt,
Wm. Ludlem, Increase Carpenter,
Rev. Abm. Ketellas, Jos. Higby,
Jonas Frederick, Andrew Oakley,
Wm. Steed, Moses Higby,
John Mills, Jacob Foster,
Isaac Bayley, Daniel Ludlam,
Increase Carpenter, Sam'l Higby, cooper,
John Cockle, Cor's Losee,
Isaac Hendrickson, Daniel Smith,
John Innes, Sr., Samuel Higby, Jr.,
Elias Bayley, Jona. Thurston,
Aaron Hendrickson, Nath'l Smith,
Robert Denton, Ephraim Marston,
John Smith, Othniel Smith,
Jacob Wright, Samuel Smith,
Nich. Smith, Sr., Wm. Creed,
Wm. Messenger, Neh. Carpenter,
Nich. Everitt, John Skidmore, Jr.,
Peter Smith, Thomas Denton,
John Brinner, Benjamin Everitt,
Daniel Tuthill, John Van Liew,
Hend'k Hendrickson, Sr. Benj. Creed,
Daniel Everitt, Isaac Mills,
John Brush, Nich. Smith, Jr.
Isaac Roads, Ben. Hinckman,
John Roads, David Lamberson,
Jonah Roads, Nathaniel Box,
Hope Roads, Wm. Creed, Jr.,
Abm. Hendrickson, Ephraim Bayley,
Hend'k Hendrickson,Jr. Oba. Smith,
Whitehead Skidmore, Jacob Carpenter,
Christopher Ryder, Neh. Carpenter,
Amos Denton, Joshua Carpenter,
Samuel Skidmore, Richard Roads,
Noah Smith, John Messenger,
Daniel Bayley, Jos. Robinson,
Walt Smith, Thos. Wiggins,
John Smith, Jacob Duryea—85
John Thurston,

NOTE.—The following persons, for some cause,
did not vote, though they had signed the Protest
against a Committee:

Aury Boerum, Geo. Fowler,
Jos. Burling, Jos. Furnan,
Geo. Bates, Robert Howell,
Abm. Colyer, John Hatchings,
Gilbert Combes, Garret Murphy,
Peter Caverly, Mervin Perry,
Jacob and John Dean, Samuel Simmons,
Jos. Dunbar, Sr., Wm. Turner,
John Grant, Chas. and Sam'l Welling.

GOV. COLDEN AT JAMAICA.

1775, May 18.—An address was presented
Lt. Gov. Colden, at Jamaica, requesting
him to intercede with Gen. Gage and the
King to stop their violent measures. His
reply was unsatisfactory, though given with
tears.

THE WHOLE COUNTY VOTE.

The Whigs, on hearing the news of the
battle of Lexington, decided to hold
another Congress. Daniel Kissam was
Chairman of a meeting held at Jamaica

May 22, 1775, which elected ten deputies to the Provincial Congress. Jos. Robinson and Jos. French were named for Jamaica, but French refused to serve. The Loyalists kept from the polls and let the election go by default.

NAMES OF COMMITTEEMEN.

Elias Baylis Chairman; Amos Denton, John Thurston, Jos. Robinson, Noah Smith, Nath'l Tuthill.

GUNPOWDER.

1775, Sep. 2nd.—Congress grant Joseph Robinson leave to receive 100 lbs. of gun powder for the use of the Jamaica militia, on his paying cash for it.

GENERAL ASSOCIATION.

The General Association was a test paper. The signers pledged themselves to stand by each other in the great struggle for their rights and to support the Congress.

DISARMING LOYALISTS.

1775, Sep. 16.—Congress having need of arms for the soldiers in Continental service, sent troops to Jamaica to impress them from those who refused to sign the General Association. Abm. Skinner, of Jamaica, reports to Congress that but few arms had been collected for want of a battalion of soldiers to intimidate the Loyalists. "The people conceal all their arms of any value, many say they know nothing about Congress and don't care for their orders, and they will blow out any man's brains that would attempt to take their arms."*

*NOTE.—Gov. Colden sent his servant around to some of the leading people, advising them to arm and defend themselves, and not deliver up their arms.

JAMAICA MINUTE MEN.

The subscribers have associated themselves as "minute men" for the defence of American liberty, and engage to be obedient to the Congress.

John Skidmore, Capt; Jacob Wright, 1st Lt; Nich. Everet, 2nd Lt; Ephraim Marston, ensign.

Privates. Cornelius and Derick Amberman; Isaac, Nehemiah, Daniel and John Baylis; John Bremner; Richard and Robert Betts; William Cebra; Peter Canile; Benjamin and Nehemiah Everet; Samuel,

Joseph, Thomas and Daniel Higbie; James Hinchman; Hendrick, Aaron and Abm. Hendrickson; John Innis; William, Nehemiah and Nathaniel Ludlum; David and Waters Lambertson; Andrew Mills; Andrew Oakley; Urias and Stephen Rider; Hope, Richard and Nathaniel Rhodes; Joseph Robinson, Richard, Nathaniel, Walter, John, Obadiah, Simeon, Sylvester, Nicholas and Benjamin Smith; Daniel Skidmore; John and Wm. Slin; Wm. and Benjamin Thurston; Thomas Wiggins; Jesse Wilson.

DEFENDERS OF LIBERTY.

1776, March 27.—A military company of 40 men associated themselves as defenders of liberty.

Ephraim Baylis Captain; Increase Carpenter, 1st Lt.; Abm. Van Osdoll, 2d Lt.; Othniel Smith, Ensign.

PETITION OF THE DISARMED.

1776, April 13.—Nath'l, Joshua, Samuel and Peter Mills, Jabez Woodruff, John Lamberson, Nich. Ludlum, Abm. Colyer, Jos. Oldfield; John Remsen, Jacob Dean and Dirck Bergen complain to Congress that having been disarmed by Col. Heard* they have since been plundered of their cattle and effects (sold at vendue for half their value), by order of Capt. Bailey, for not appearing in arms (when they had none), nor answering to their names at a training.

*NOTE.—At 3 different times American Soldiers had marched into Jamaica, to disarm the Loyalists.

DELINQUENTS ADVERTISED.

1776, June 13.—Capt. Ephraim Bayley publishes in a New York Paper that "Nicholas Ludlum, Sr. and Jr., Jos. Oldfield, John Remsen, and Jabez Woodruff having thrice neglected to attend the times and places appointed for military exercise and having thrice been fined, are hereby advertised and held up as enemies to their country."

NO INSULTS TO CONGRESS.

1776, April 26.—All friends of American liberty in Jamaica are entreated to aid the Committee. Should any officers in the service of Congress, meet with insults in the discharge of their duties the offenders will be treated as enemies to their country.

ELIAS BAYLIS, Chairman.

POWDER.

1776, May 28.—Congress order 100 lbs. gun powder to be delivered to Capt. Baylis to be distributed to those well affected to the American cause.

SUSPICIOUS CHARACTERS.

1776, May 15.—No person shall move into Jamaica without producing a certificate from the Committee where he last resided, that he is a friend of the American cause. All suspicious persons passing through the town, will be arrested for examination. By order of the Committee.

ELIAS BAYLIS, Chairman.

1776, May 28.—Captain Thos. Harriot, of Jamaica, having refused to take the Continental money, is held up by order of Congress as an enemy to his country.

PAY ROLL.

Pay roll of the Jamaica militia (from July 25th to Aug. 31, 1776) stationed on the shores south side of Jamaica* and at New York Ferry. £149.2.10 due.

Wm. Ludlum, Captain, $26⅔ per month.
Increase Carpenter, 1st Lt. $18 per month.
Ephraim Marstin 2d Lt. $18   "   "
Benj. Thurston, 1st Serg't. $8   "   "
Hend'k. Hendrickson 2d Serg't. $8 per month.
Oba. Smith Corporal $7⅓ per month.
Noah Smith, Corporal $7⅓   "   "
Nich. Lamberson, Drummer, $7⅓ per month.
Bernardus Ryder, Fifer, $7⅓ per month.

PRIVATES.—$6⅔ per month.

Samuel Higbie,	Nicholas Wortman,
John Innes,	John Smith,
Isaac Van Osdol,	Neh. Carpenter, bl'ksmith,
Aaron Hendrickson,	Henry Wiggins,
Stephen Rider,	Nehemiah Smith,
Nehemiah Ludlum,	John Bailey,
Nehemiah Bailey,	Lawrence Stivers,
Wm. Stine,	Peter Frederick,
Nich. Lamberson,	H. Hendrickson, bl'ksm'th.
Cornelius Creed,	Abm. Golder,
Sylvester Smith,	Richard Betts,
Thomas Brady,	Charles Smith,
— MacLean,	Abm. Ditmars,
John Bennet,	Rem Remsen,
John Bishop.	

☞ Drafted but not delivered: Benj. Whitehead, Jos. Dunbar, and Peter Mills.

*NOTE.—Isaiah Doxsey says the Americans had a force stationed with pitched tents at Far Rockaway. Nelly Cornell, looking out of an upper story window, called to the Captain and told him she "saw trees rising from the ocean." He looked, and then called another officer, and said: "That's the British fleet, down with the tents, and let's be off to the Ferry." Wagons were then impressed to convey the baggage, and the cattle were driven off.

NOTE.—After the defeat of the Americans at Brooklyn this company was disbanded, and the men mostly returned to their homes.

NAMING CHILDREN.

The Presbyterians of Jamaica were not slow in honoring our Revolutionary heroes, for we find, Jan. 28, 1776, a child baptized *John Hancock* Marston, and on July 24th, another named *George Washington* Smith. As an offset, we find one named (1780) *Beloyal* Livingston.

THE CENTENNIAL HISTORY OF JAMAICA.

DEPUTIES.

1775, Nov. 7.—An election for Deputies to the Provincial Congress was again held at Jamaica. The polls were kept open from Tuesday till Saturday, at 5 o'clock afternoon. Seven were nominated, Waters Smith for Jamaica. The whole county voted, and the poll stood 221 for Deputies, and 747 against. So Queens county had no representation in the Congress till May 14th 1776.

The names of those who voted against Deputies were printed in two N. Y. papers, so that they might be held up to the public contempt, and that the whigs might shun all dealings or intercouse with them.

The Asia, a British ship of war, lay off Rockaway, and supplied the disaffected with arms and ammunition, and also received fresh provision from the farmers. Congress issued this handbill:

1775, Dec. 13.—Whereas some disaffected persons in Queens couty have been supplied with arms from the Asia, ship of war, and are arraying themselves to oppose the measures taken by the United Colonies for their just rights, it is ordered that Captain Benj. Whitehead, Dr. Chas. Arden, Capt. Jos. French and Capt. Johannes Polhemus, all of Jamaica, appear before this Congress on the 19th inst., to give satisfaction in the premises; and that they be protected from insult, coming and returning.

DISAFFECTED PERSONS IN JAMAICA.

The Whig Committee sent to the Congress in N. Y. the following list of suspicious characters (June 21, 1776), who kept in and about Jamaica.

1. Dr. Chas. Arden.—He instigated the Tories to sign against having a Congress or Committee.
2. Capt. Ben. Whitehead, late Supervisor. He refused to communicate to the people of Jamaica the letters he received from the Whig Committee of N. Y.

3. Alex. Wallace, merchant of N. Y. but now lives in Waters Smith's house.
4. Geo. Bethnue, from Boston. He is intimate with Arden and Whitehead.
5. Samuel Martin from Antigua. He lives in Oba. Mill's house, and associates with Jas. Depeyster.
6. Chas. McEvers, formerly a stamp-officer. He lives in John Troup's house.
7, 8, and 9. Thos. and Fleming Colgan, and John W. Livingston, Jr. They often go on Creed's hill to look out for the British fleet expected off Sandy Hook.
10 and 11. John and Wm. Dunbar shut themselves up and refused to train or pay their fines.
12. George Folliot, merchant from N. Y. He lives at Juques Johnson's, Fresh Meadow.
13. Theophylact Bache, of Flatbush. He comes to Alex. Wallace's at Jamaica.
14. James Depeyster.—He lives next to Wm. Betts and is said to be a dangerous Tory. His son has been pursued several times, but can't be taken.

HUNTING TORIES.

1776, June 21.—The loyalists, when warned to train in the militia companies, refused to appear, and often hid away in the woods and swamps. They were sometimes hunted out.

I will read an order :

Lt. THOS. MITCHELL :

You are hereby ordered to march your company into Capt. Peter Nostrand's district, and assist him to bring the 2-3 defaulters of his company, or such as you can find, to Samuel Nicoll's, and there secure them. JOHN SANDS, Col.

Stephen Rider, with other Jamaica minute men, was ordered to a swamp at the head of Dorlon's mill pond, in Hempstead. He climed up an oak tree to reconnoitre, when a ball whistled by his head. He saw by the smoke whence it came. He called for a loaded gun which was handed up to him, and firing at a venture, hit a lad of 18, named Geo. Smith, just below the shoulder. The party surrendered, and were brought to Jamaica jail. After the British possession of L. I., Rider was arrested for this and suffered great hardships in the Provost prison, and was heavily fined.

1776, June 24.—An election of Delegates to Congress was held at Jamaica, Rev. Abm. Keteltas and Waters Smith were nominated for Jamaica.

In Congress, John Jay moved that :

WHEREAS, Rev. Abm. Keteltas has been solemnly devoted to the service of God and the cure of souls, he has good right to claim exemption from all such employments as would divert his mind from that kingdom which is not of this world.

Mr. Keteltas was excused by a vote of 23 to 18 from service in Congress.

The Declaration of Independence was voted July 4th, and sent with a letter from John Hancock, but not acted on by the N. Y. Provincial Congress till July 9th, when they ordered it published by beat of drum, and 500 copies in hand bills to be circulated in the several counties of the State. It was read at the head of every military company in Queens county.

I have heard my father (J. O.) say he read it aloud at noon-spell to the family, who were all called together to hear it.

July 20—Congress order the live stock south of the Ridge of Hills on L. I. to be driven toward Hempstead Plains, in order to keep it out of the hands of the enemy, whose fleet was daily expected off Sandy Hook.

NEW YORK, July the 3d, 1776.

To Coll. John Sands, Esqr.:

SIR—I have this day waited upon his Excellency, General Washington, relating to removing the cattle, horses and sheep on the south side of Queens county, according to resolve of Congress and the General officers of the army. His opinion is that the Commanding officers and Committee of the county order it immediately done. He further declared that in case the Tories made any resistance he would send a number of his men with orders to shoot all the creatures, and also those who hindered the execution of said resolves within the limits therein prescribed. The Commissary of the Army engaged to me that he would pay the full value for the fat cattle and sheep to the owners, provided they would drive them within General Green's lines in Brooklyn. Proper care will be taken as to valuing said creatures. Time will not permit us to make any delay.

I am, sir, your very humble servant,
JEROMUS REMSEN, Jr.

WHITE PLAINS, July 20th, 1776.

SIR—I have received orders from Congress to give orders to all the Commanding officers of my Brigade to hold themselves in readiness. Sir, you are, therefore, directed to keep the Regiment under your command in readiness to march on the shortest notice with five days provision, to any part of Long Island, where you shall be directed, for the defence of the same. I am, sir, your humble sarvant,

NATH'L WOODHULL, Brig. Gen'l.
To. Col. Sands.

WOODHULL.

Gen. Woodhull had command of the American party that were driving off the live stock ; and therefore the British were eager to overtake and capture him, and recover the cattle.

Hence, on Aug. 28th the day after the defeat of the American army at Brooklyn, a detachment of the 17th Light Dragoons galloped into the village of Jamaica, amid thunder, lightning and rain, in pursuit of Woodhull's party. He was at Jamaica with only 90 men. Those he ordered to move eastward, driving the stock before them. He waited at Jamaica for further orders from Congress. At last he moved slowly on to Carpenter's tavern, 2 miles east of Jamaica. It is supposed he sought temporary shelter there from a shower. But as he came out of the house to remount his horse, and had his hand on the reins, the British Light horse galloped up. They cried out: "surrender you d——d Rebel," say "God save the King." As he did not do this, but tendered his sword, they showered their sabre blows on his head and his arm, as it was uplifted, to ward off the strokes.

They then quickly mounted him on horse back behind one of the troopers, bleeding as he was, and hurried back to Jamaica, where his wounds were dressed, and he was kept under guard. His shirt sleeve cut with seven gashes, and his hat slashed in many places, were long preserved in his family.

Next day, with other prisoners, Woodhull was taken to a prison ship at New Utrecht. He was so weak that he was allowed to ride in a chaise with David Lamberson. His arm cut in the elbow joint, soon mortified, and was taken off by Dr. Bailey, of the British service. But he soon died, and his wife, who was with him in his last moments, conveyed his embalmed body to Mastic, where it was interred on his farm, about the 23d of September.

SUBMISSION.

When the American army abandoned L. I., to the enemy the more active Whigs fled. Rev. Messrs. Keteltas and Froeligh crossed to the Main as did John I. Skidmore, Increase Carpenter and others. The property of those who fled was seized by the British authorities. But most of the Whigs staid at home with their families, and took their chance. The more obnoxious were arrested and taken to the British camp in Kings county. Among these were Elias Baylis, an aged and blind man, an Elder in the Presbyterian Chnrch, David Lamberson, Abm. Ditmars, Robart Hinchman, John Thurston and others.

The more quiet whigs were not disturbed. They took the oath of allegiance to the Crown, signed a paper of submission, and prayed to be restored to the Royal favor, and wore a red ribbon on their hats.

Some whigs who did not come promptly forward and get a protection paper from the British General, were informed against by their malicious neighbors, and hurried off to the Provost prison in N. Y., where, by the inhumanity of Cunningham, the Provost Marshal, they suffered great privations, and some even died.

All whigs were notified that if they expected any indulgence from the Crown they must make proof of their attachment to the Royal cause, by supplying fresh provisions, cattle, grain &c., for the army.

Several of the more active Loyalists of Jamaica, made offers of their services to the British; and were sent into Suffolk county to collect wagons and horses, live stock, forage and the like for Howe's army. Among these were Joshua and Hope Mills, and John Dunbar.

FARM PRODUCE.

The farmers had to reserve their hay, grain, wood, &c., for the British army, and it had to be sold at prices fixed by a Proclamation of the British commandant.

In Sep. 1776, a printed circular (with blanks to be filled up), was left with each farmer:

"You are hereby ordered to preserve for the King's use 3 loads of hay, 50 bushels of wheat, 50 of oats, 50 of rye, 50 of barley, 50 of Indian corn, and all your wheat and rye straw, and not to dispose of the same, but to an order in writing from Major John Morrison, Commissary for forage, as you will answer the contrary at your peril."

In 1780, '81 and '82, each town was required to furnish able-bodied horses for the army. The horses were brought to Jamaica, delivered to the Commissary General, and after inspection, and valuation, paid for.

IMPRESSMENTS.

Impressing teams was very annoying. If in your wagon going to church, to a funeral, or to mill, or on any other urgent business, you were liable to be stopped and forced away with your team on the King's service.

☞ Here is one of those little tickets, so dreaded by the farmers:

FLUSHING, 26th Sep. 1776.

To Luke Bergen:
Press two wagons for the service of the Light Dragoons.
S. BIRCH, Lt. Col.

HEAD QUARTERS.

Jamaica being somewhat central, was usually the Head Quarters of the British commandants of L. I., Gen. Oliver Delancey, Tryon and others.

The street was patrolled, day and night, so that all stragglers, deserters and runaway negroes were liable to be arrested and brought before the Commandant for examination.

An American Sailor having escaped from the Prison ship at the Wallabout had to pass thro' this village. He saw a negro boy driving cattle along the road, so he picked up a stick and commenced hurrying up the cows as if he was one of the drivers. The trick succeeded, and he passed by the patrol unnoticed. At another time going by a corn field he saw at a distance some soldiers approaching. He at once jumped over the fence into the field and began to right up the stocks of corn, as if they had fallen apart. The soldiers passed on without hailing him, supposing him to be a farm laborer.

SOLDIERS.

In the Summer season the British troops were out on expeditions to various places on the Main; as to Connecticut, Jersey, the Carolinas, Georgia, &c., but in the Winter they quartered on L. I., and Jamaica had her full share. Huts were dug into the side hills north of Jamaica, and covered with boards, thatch and sods.

Some soldiers were billeted* on the house holders. The first notice they had was: "Madam, we have come to take a billet on your house," and they chalked on the door the number of soldiers each house must receive, usually about half the house was taken. Then, to save your fences, you must keep a big wood pile at the door, for soldiers were very handy with their hatchets, and would convert fencing stuff into fuel without hesitation.

*NOTE.—Billeting is so called from the *billet* or ticket that the soldiers exhibited to the master of the house, as their warrant to occupy a part of it.

The highest officers had a house to themselves, especially one that had been deserted by its Whig owner. Thus General

Skinner had the house of Rev. Mr. Keteltas. Rev. Mr. Bowden occupied the Dutch parsonage.

Among British officers who were quartered in Jamaica were General Oliver Delancey, who had command of all the Island, Gen'l Tryon, Lord Rawdon, Sir Wm. Erskine, Lord Cornwallis.

The English officers expected the utmost reverence from all who came in their presence. Even if a farmer should meet one in the street and forget to pull off his hat he might expect a caning.

In the fall of 1780 one Capt. Crow, a British half pay officer, sent his servant to Derick Amberman's mill for some flour. The miller, half joking, bid the servant tell his master to send the money with his bag next time, as he could trust him no longer. This message so enraged the officer that he at once mounted his horse and rode to the mill, and calling the miller out, beat him on the head with a loaded whip till he fell to the earth, when a brother officer ran him thro' with a sword.

While this assault was going on, a wagon with several people in it came along who would have assisted the miller, but the officer bid them in *the King's name* to stand; and such was their timidity that they dared not lift a hand to help him. The miller died of his wounds; and it is not known that the officers were punished.

Recruiting offices were established here.

Soldiers were billeted in almost every house in Jamaica. When the soldiers had behaved well, had not stolen too much, and had treated the farmers civilly, a parting address was often presented them. Thus 26 of the Loyal inhabitants of Foster's Meadow and Springfield, being impressed with gratitude gave thanks to Tarlton's British Legion that wintered there in 1781–'82. The soldiers not to be outdone in courtesy, in their reply, wish that the farmers' "fields may yield them a most plentiful harvest, and that their flocks may bring forth in abundance."

This same Col. Tarlton when leaving Suffolk county was guilty of great rapacity in carrying off the produce of the whigs.

He took boards off their barns (Nov. 3,

1777), to build barracks for his soldiers. A marketman had bought 70 fowls which he had dressed to carry to market in N. Y. for the Christmas Holidays. Tarlton took *all* these from him and also two barrels of new cider to wash them down. From another farmer he carried off 3 hogs. At one time (Oct. 20, 1779), he was out on a party of pleasure, shooting grouse, he came to a house when seeing a cow at pasture in a lot he took her out and had her killed for his troops. On another occasion (Oct. 7, 1779), he took a heifer and had her killed for the use of his "sick soldiers," as he said.

He took 40 lbs. butter and poultry from another farmer (Nov. 1777), and would give neither receipt nor pay.

In 1780 he took a fat beast worth £25 and Dec. 3, 1778, as he was marching from Smithtown to Jericho, he carried off four fat hogs from a farmer's pen, worth £30.

PASSES.

Persons travelling without a pass were liable to be arrested by the British patroles. Hence when an officer impressed a farmer to go on any errand or business for him, he gave him a pass.

I will read a few of the samples:

JAMAICA, 29th Aug., 1776.

Permit Isaac Bennet to pass and repass without molestation. WILL. ERSKINE, Brig. Gen.

CEDAR SWAMP, June 10, 1782.

The bearer, a negro man, being employed in carting provisions for the corps of Yagers is permitted to pass to Flushing, Bayside, unmolested.

OCHSE, Lt. Ad'jt Yager's.

1782, June 8th.

Permit the bearer hereof, Silas Pettit, of Hempstead, to pass to New York and return. By order of

BENJ HEWLETT,

Capt. Queens County Militia.

HEMPSTEAD, Jan. 4, 1777.

Permit the bearer hereof, Mr. Sam'l Pettit, jr., to pass without hinderance to New York Island, and thence to N.J., or until he find his wagon and horses, now in His Majesty's service, as he has always acted as a friend to Gov't.

S. CLOWES,

a Justice of the Peace in Queens Co.

ENJOYMENTS.

Tho' the farmers and laboring classes had to live frugally and on homely fare, different was it with the British officers. They spent their money freely, and loved good eating and drinking. Here is a note from an officer to a farmer:

Sir: If you can get me a good quarter of veal, or a good pig, or half a dozen good chickens, pray do so; for I can't live on salt meat every day, and you'll oblige Yours, Cor's VAN HORNE.

The standing toast at an officer's table was "a long, and a moderate war."

The out door amusements were fox hunting, shooting grouse and other game, horse-racing, cricket matches, hurling matches billards, cards &c. They indulged in music also, for we read of pianos, harpsichords, organs, &c., beside military bands.

Some of the officers had their *ladies* with them; others married American girls. Some of the common soldiers brought their wives with them, from the old country, especially the Hessians and Scotch. Their children were baptized in the Presbyterian church. On one occasion the sexton had forgot to have the water ready and was going to get some, when the mother pulled a bottle out of her pocket and said "here's water." This was poured into the baptismal basin.

BALLS AND DANCES.

While the British officers were in Jamaica every occasion for amusement, fun and frolic was improved. Thus Oct. 26th was the anniversary of the accession of George III. to the throne. So there must be a good time. Accordingly we read this advertisement in the papers (1779):

"Tickets for the *Accession Ball* for the inhabitants of Jamaica, and the officers quartered there, are now being issued. A grand band of music will be wanted."

1780, March 17.—A munificent entertainment was given by Lord Rawdon, Colonel of the volunteers of Ireland, to his regiment quartered at Jamaica, in honor of St. Patrick, the tutelar saint of Ireland. Song by Barny Thompson, piper of the regiment. Here follow a few lines of the song:

"So Yankees keep off, or you'll soon learn your error,
For Paddy shall prostrate lay every foe."

" Hand in hand! Let's carol the chorus,
As long as the blessings of Ireland hang o'er us,
The crest of *rebellion* shall tremble before us,
Like brothers, while we thus march hand in hand.'

TAVERNS.

There were several taverns in Jamaica, and they were well supported, as British gold was abundant. They were named after the pictures on their sign-boards, as the Half Moon tavern, the Queen's Head, the King's Arms, the Gen. Amherst, &c.

Here follow a couple of advertisements:

1779, July 10.—"Wm. Betts has opened the tavern (formerly kept by John Comes), the Gen. Amherst, where he has provided choice liquors. Dinner on the shortest notice, and good stabling."

1781, May 12.—"Thos. Rochford, of the Queen's Head, has a house of 8 rooms. He begs leave to inform the ladies and gentlemen that he has an elegant garden—a tea garden—with arbors, bowers, alcoves, grottos, statues of Naids, dryads, hamadryads, &c., &c. He has a stock of good liquors, and can, at any time, furnish genteel dinners. The ladies and gentlemen who choose to make an excursion from N. Y. to the pleasant village of Jamaica (so remarkable for the salubrity of its air), may depend on good cheer at his house, and the utmost attention."

The drinks at a tavern were: Jamaica and Antigua spirits, sangaree, negus, punch, lemonade, slings, (i. e. spirits and water sweetened with loaf sugar and nutmeg grated in it); for the ladies there would be milk punch, tea, coffee and chocolate, and wines. The fashion of Brandy drinking was introduced by the French officers.

NOTE—The officers sometimes had a silver strainer to run the punch through before they drank it. They were fond of taking a tiff of punch.

STAGES.

While the British were in occupation of Jamaica, stages to N. Y. were in great demand, and had odd sounding names.

1777, Oct. 6.—The new *Stage wagon* will set out from Hope Mills at 7 o'clock on Monday, Wednesday and Saturday mornings for Brooklyn ferry and return on same days. For freight or passage apply to the public's humble servant, Hope Mills.

N. B. Proper care taken of all the letters and newspapers.*

1779, May 26.—Loosley & Elms propose to run a *Caravan* to Jamaica and back to Brooklyn ferry on Tuesdays, Thursdays and Sundays.

1781, March.—Benjamin Creed's Jamaica and Brooklyn Hall stage *Machine*, 6/ a passage. He will not be answerable for any money, plate or jewels, unless they are entered on his book and paid for.

1782, Oct. 3.—New *Flying Machine* on steel springs, Thursday, Sunday and Tuesday from Brooklyn at 8 o'clock to Jamaica, and return same evening. Breakfasting at Brooklyn on stage mornings.

*NOTE.—Jamaica had no mail till 1800, when Eliphalet Wickes was appointed postmaster.

PERMITS.

Shopping had to be done in Revolutionary times as well as now. The ladies sometimes went to the City, tho' there were plenty of good stores in Jamaica. But no goods could be brought out of N. Y. without a permit. I have an old one which I will read:

"Pursuant to His Excellency, Sir. Wm. Howe's proclamation, permission is hereby given to Aaron Van Nostrand to cart to Jamaica, one bushel salt, he having complied with the directions.
JOHN NUGENT, Dep. Supt."

The following is a list of articles a lady had permision to bring out of the city:

14 lbs. Sugar,
½ cwt. Rice,
10 yds. Calico,
7 yds. Russet,
6 yds. Durant,
1 lb Whalebone,
1 lb Pepper,
2 galls. Molasses,
2 galls. Rum,
1 lb tea,
1 lb Coffee,
1 lb Chocolate,
1 bush. Salt,
1 pair Gloves.

The restriction put on taking goods out of N. Y. was intended to prevent smuggling from L. I. across the Sound to Conn. Imported goods were scarce on the Main and commanded a high price.

AARON VAN NOSTRAND

was an important character in Jamaica, in his day. He was a turner by trade, and made chairs and spinning wheels. He also acted as clerk and sexton of the English Church. For 47 years he was grave digger, and rang the funeral bells. He was gathered to his fathers, Jan. 23d, 1822, at the age of 84. He left a record book of all the interments in Grace Church yard from 1773 to 1820, and of all the funeral bells he rang for those buried elsewhere. This book I gave to Parson Johnson, but at his death was cast aside as useless trash. I give a sample of bills from it:

JAMAICA, Oct. 24, 1780.

General DELANCEY,
To Grace Church, Dr.:
To digging a grave for Major Waller.....£0.10
" a funeral bell............................. 0.5
" use of the church pall................. 0.4
" inviting and attending the funeral..... 0.16
1776, April 21—Taking up the floor and putting it down, for Mrs. Coigan (who was buried in the church), 6 shillings.
1776, Oct. 1—Jos. Horsfield, half funeral bell for his child, 2s. 6d.
1778, July 8—For inviting to Jos. Read's funeral, and grog to the carriers, 10s.
Four carrers at 8s. each.

1778, Dec. 25—Charles McEvers, inviting and attending funeral, 12s.; bell 5s., use of pall 8s.; six carriers £2.8.

In 1781, Aug. 16th, Aaron Van Nostrand was directed to warn the inhabitants of Jamaica to work on the road leading to Flushing, and put it in good order, and to fine delinquents 8 shilling a day each.

In 1782, Oct. 16th, he was appointed Marshall of the Police and Inspector of the weight and quality of bread in Jamaica, with directions to inspect the several bake houses once a week in order to examine the bread.

BEAVER POND.

The Green southeast side of Beaver Pond was a mustering and training ground for the militia. There was a race course around it; the circuit being precisely one mile.

Advertisements like these occur in the New York papers:

RACES.

1778, Oct. 14—Purse of 20 guineas, around Beaver Pond.

1779, Oct. 26—Jamaica Races, 3 heats, twice round the course at Beaver Pond, each heat. Purse 20 guineas.

1782, Oct. 19—A Purse of £50, to be run for around Beaver Pond, the best 2 in 3 one mile heats. One guinea entrance. Free for any horse except Mercury, Slow and Easy, and Goldfinder.

1783, June 28—A purse of 100 guineas is to be run for Wednesday next, around Beaver Pond, by the noted mare Calfskin, and the noted horse Lofty from Boston.

The Green was the scene of an execution Nov. 12, 1784. Two persons Wm. Guthrie and Jos. Alexander had robbed Thos. Thorne, of Cow Neck, of a silver tankard * and other articles. The old Jail standing at Mr. Peck's Pharmacy, had been destroyed by the British. So the prisoners were kept in the Bridewell, in N. Y. and brought up to Jamaica for trial by an escort of Soldiers. The Court was held in the Presbyterian Church. The convicts were taken to the gallows in a wagon each seated on his own coffin. Here follow some items of the cost of the execution:

Queens County, to Nehemiah Hinchman, Dr.:

	£.	s.
For making the gallows, and my trouble	0	16
Timber and spikes	1	5
Blacksmith's work	0	17
2 carpenters, 4 days each	4	16
Wagon and horses to take the gallows to the Pond	0	4

Help in raising the gallows	0	
Wm. Thurston, for staples	0	18
2 coffins, each 16s	1	12
Rope to hang with, and handkerchiefs to tie over their eyes	0	14
Sheriff's fees for hanging	12	0
Digging the graves	0	18
Ringing the bell for the procession to move and cleaning the church when the trial was held	1	16

*NOTE.—This tankard which was the means of convicting the criminals, was on exhibition at the late Queens County Fair. It is yet preserved as an heir-loom in the family of Henry T. Hewlett.

COURTS.

For the years of British occupation, there were no Courts, but military rule prevailed. The King's Justices of the Peace held over, and their decisions were backed by the soldiery. Court Martials were the only tribunal to which the injured could resort till July 15, 1780, when an office of Police (as it was called), was established at Jamaica, and George D. Ludlow appointed Superintendent. His jurisdiction extended over the Island. David Colden was his assistant, and James Creighton, Secretary.

MINISTERS.

In the English church was the Rev. Joshua Bloomer. When the Whigs ordered him, in July 1776, to omit the prayers for the King, he closed his church for 5 weeks, and did not perform services till the British got possession. He had once been in the army and had been a trader and failed, but on receiving a legacy he paid off all his indebtedness. He once married a rich couple, and next day some one asked him what fee he got; "O, I forgot all about it," (said he). "It must be in my other coat pocket." It proved to be 3 guineas wrapped in a piece of paper. He died unmarried, June 23, 1790, and was buried in the church.

"He sleeps in chancel, not a stone records His name, his fame, his actions or his words."

In the Presbyterian Church was Rev. Mr. Burnet. He was almost the only Presbyterian minister who favored the British cause. He remained in Jamaica all thro' the war and performed religious services. He saved the church from desecration. When the enemy first entered Jamaica, some loyal youngsters mounted into the belfry with a rope and saw and began to saw off the posts of the steeple, but Mr. Burnet hastened to the British commandant, and soon had a stop put to their proceedings. Yet when peace came the Whigs of his congregation forced him to leave.

Froeligh, the Dutch minister, was a rampant Whig, and had to flee when the enemy approached Jamaica, and never returned to take charge of his church. He used to pray that God's lightning would strike the British ships and sink their soldiers in the sea, so that they might not set hostile feet on our shores. A more moderate Whig minister used to pray that the British soldiers might speedily return by the way they came.

CHURCHES.

The Dutch church was taken by the British, and used as a store house. The pulpit was left, but the pews and floors were taken out and used for building huts and barracks for the soldiers. Here often on Sundays, wagons drove up for the weekly allowance of pork, rum, flour, peas, &c., which were carted to various parts of the Island.

The Dutch people worshipped by permission in the Episcopal church. Their own minister had fled from the Island, but Domines Rubell and Schoonmaker, from Flatbush, occasionally officiated, and baptized the children. Rubell was a staunch Royalist, and always prayed for King Geo. III., Queen Charlotte, the princes and princesses of the Royal family, and the Parliament. He was a rotund, jolly little parson and was too fond of the pleasures of the table.

SALES BY AUCTION.

When the evacuation of Jamaica, by the British was drawing near auction sales were frequent.

The British government sold warlike stores:

1782, July 29. To be sold by auction at Jamaica, sundry damaged provisions, consisting of pork, peas and butter.

1782 Sep. 25. To be sold at Jamaica, several high bred stallions, among them Lofty and Brutus, belonging to British cavalry officers, both capital 4 mile horses, also Comus and 2 or 3 Capital hunters. To be seen at Mr. Betts', Queen's Head tavern.

1783 April 15. To be sold at Jamaica, 40 excellent dragoon horses in high condition belonging to cavalry officers.

1783, July 19. Several horses of the 17th Light Dragoons to be sold at Jamaica.

Several stores were set up in Jamaica during the war. These also were discontinued, and sold out at auction, viz.

Ray and Fitzsimmons.

Alex'r Haire who kept the noted White store at Little Plains; Michael Price who had the best stand within the British lines, went to England.

Hart and Chaloner failed—whole stock sold, consisting of dry goods, china and earthern ware and groceries.

Cunningham, Scott and Co., Alexander McAuley and Co., Malcolm Morrison and Wm. Lanman.

Several private families going into exile also sold out their furniture, as we see by their advertisements:

1778—Auction, Sept. 21st, of all the household furniture of Mr. Simeon Lugrin, * Jamaica. Sale to begin at 10 o'clock in the morning.

N. B. To be sold sametime a fine-toned double harpsichord.

* He was school master at Burton, Nova Scotia from 1799 to 1806.

1782, Aug. 21.—Capt. Wm. Wade, intending for Ireland per first fleet, will sell at vendue a Piano, Mahogany chairs, phaeton, &c.

1783, March 21—Public Auction at the office of Police ., mahogany tables and chairs, beds and bedsteads, an elegant 8 day clock, glass, china, pewter and earthenware, and some plate, kitchen utensils. Also a likely negro wench, with her male child, and a riding mare. GEO. DUNCAN LUDLOW.

1784, Sep. 17—The household furniture, farming utensils, riding chair, horses and cows of Joseph French to be sold at auction.

FUEL.

1777, Nov. 24.—A town meeting was held to provide fire wood and other necessary articles for the use of the Hospital and Guard house in Jamaica; and it was voted (1) that all householders who have soldiers billeted on them be excepted from contributing; (2) that the following persons be appointed Trustees for the above purpose, viz: John Polhemus for the Western district; John Lamberson and John Doughty for Springfield; Jacamiah Valentine for the Eastern district, and Dowe Ditmars for the Southern district; and (3) that Edward Willett be appointed to inspect the wood and give certificates.

SLAVES.

In the disorder and lawlessness that followed on the British occupation, the slaves caught the infection, became insubordinate, and in search of adventures abandoned their masters. Even as early as March 6th 1775, we find this startling paragraph in the New York *Mercury.* "Several of the negroes at Jamaica, L. I., we hear, were last week committed to the gaol there for a conspiracy to destroy the whites. Most of the slaves for many miles round, 'tis said, are concerned in this plot." Letting this pass for a *canard*, we give some advertisements of the runaways:

1777, May 26.—$4 *Reward*—Ran away from Capt. Thos. Harriot, Jamaica South, a negro bred to the sea. He had on a beaver hat cocked, homespun trowsers, short gray coat with brass buttons. Masters of vessels are desired not to ship him.

1779, Feb. 27.—$6 *Reward*—Ran away from Benj. Smith, Jamaica, Tom. He had on a gray short coat, belt waistcoat yellow metal buttons, buff breeches, and white worsted stockings." 'Tis thought he will try to go out in some privateer.

1780, June, 4—*Two guineas Reward*—Ran away from John Amberman, a negro man Will, with thick lips. He had on corduroy breeches.

1781, May 16.—$10 *Reward*—Ran away from Ray & Fitzsimmons, a negro Hercules. He had on velvet plush breeches, and is apt to stutter on a surprise; and with him a large fat young wench, with three cuts on each cheek, a slave of Col. Linsing, late from Charleston.

1782, June 12.—$10 *Reward*—Ran away from Dowe Ditmars, a negro boy Frank. He took a blue broadcloth coat and jacket, and a new castor hat. It is imagined he intends going on board some privateer

1783, Sep. 10.—Ran away from Edward Bardin, Sam, a mulatto, who had on a striped jacket and trowsers made of bed tick. He carried off a red waistcoat, buckskin breeches and two pair of white breeches.

ROBBERIES.

The British commandant did what he could to prevent the soldiers and others from plundering at night, and severely punished the offenders whenever they could be detected. Many farmers, however, could find no redress.

Wm. Ludlum, in the Bog lots, was robbed of linen, clothing, &c. Some money hid behind the chimney escaped the search of the robbers, who broke in a panel of the door with a huge stone.

John Williamson was tortured and robbed of £300 hid under the hearthstone. The same gang the next night broke into Wm. Creed's house, where a Highlander slept as a safe-guard, who beat them off and killed one.*

The widow Mills' house, upper end of Springfield, was broke into, but she escaped and sounded an alarm. The robbers, tho' fired on by the neighbors, escaped. A patrol was then set from the head of Springfield to Amberman's gate on the Rockaway road. 'Squire B. Everett was severely abused by robbers before he could be induced to disclose his hidden treasure, about $250.

*Note.—Wm. Creed was a Whig and suffered on that account. Some British soldiers came to his house to drive off his cows. The wife begged the officer to leave them. He replied, "Why, madam, they belong to the Crown," and carried them away. At another time the dragoons turned their horses into his oats just as it was in head. He had much of his wood cut.

HORSE STEALING.

Beside petty thefts by night, horse stealing was prevalent. We give a few instances:

1777—A guinea reward and charges paid—Stolen or strayed in the night of Nov. 20, from the pasture of Rev. Mr. John Bowden a dark gray mare.

1777, Dec. 6.—$20 *Reward*—Lost two black mares, by Capt. Jacob Smith, of the 1st company of the 1st battalion of Delancey's Brigade at Jamaica.

1778, Jan. 31.—Stolen or strayed from the pasture of Dr. Charlton, a black mare.

1778.—$3 *Reward*—Stolen or strayed, May 15, out of Thos. Harriot's pasture, a mouse-colored cow and 2 yearlings, with the broad arrow marked on each.

1779.—$10 *Reward*—Stolen in the night of Feb. 24, out of Major Thos. Bowden's stable, a sorrel horse, his mane lying on the mounting side, the property of Rev. John Bowden.

Mr. Bowden was an Assistant Minister of Trinity Church, N. Y. till March 14, 1777, when he removed to Jamaica and occupied the Parsonge house abandoned by Frocleigh, the Dutch minister.

HAY.

1780, July 1.—Gov. Robertson assures the farmers that if they bring to the British Commissary two thirds of their first grass, they may keep the other third. Certificates of hay and cartage paid for on presentation.

Benj. Nostrand once told me he stood on Bett's stoop and counted 110 wagon loads of hay passing by one after the other to New York.

LOTTERIES.

1778—"A lottery for raising £780 toward purchasing a globe for the established church in the parish of Jamaica, will be drawn under the inspection of persons of character." From the proceeds of this lottery, Wm. Creed's farm of 70 acres nearly a mile westward of the village was bought. 1782, June 3—Tickets for the Brooklyn Hall Charity Lottery for the relief of refugees, poor soldiers &c., for sale at Edward Bardin's inn, Jamaica.

EXCURSIONS.

1782 Sept. 18.—An elegant carriage for the accommodation of 6 or 8 ladies and gentlemen from Mr. Hill's, Brooklyn ferry to any part of L. I. for $6 per day. Performed by Benj. Creed.

A party of British officers made a pleasure excursion to Success Pond when Capt. Dickson was drowned while bathing. His remains were brought back to Jamaica and interred on the east side of Grace Church. He is the only British officer who has a stone over his grave.

HORSES.

1781, May 5.—Col. Hamilton again reminds the Captains of Queens county that the horses demanded by the Quartermaster General for his Majesty's immediate service, are to be delivered on Wednesday, 9th inst., at Jamaica, by 9 o'clock in the morning. Each company of foot (19 in all), is to furnish nine horses, and each troop of horse is to furnish four horses. None but strong young horses will pass inspection.

WOOD.

1780, June 21.—" Agreeable to Governor Robertson's proclamation, the Captains of Queens county militia will meet on Saturday, at the house of Wm. Betts, tavern keeper in Jamaica, at 11 o'clock forenoon, to concert measures for furnishing fuel." *N. B. Wood cutters will meet with the best encouragement by applying to Mr. Betts.

*NOTE.—About 4,500 cords of wood was annually required of Queens county for the use of the British army in and about New York.

MILITIA UNIFORM.

1780, Feb. 7.—Col. Hamilton desires that the officers of the regiment of loyal Queens county, will provide themselves with a uniform. It is to be a scarlet coat faced with blue, with white lining, white waistcoat and breeches, and silver buttons with a silver epaulet, a well cocked hat with silver buttons and loops, and silver hat band. Any officer appearing on duty without regimentals or side arms may depend on being fined half a joe for the entertainment of their brother officers.

SAMUEL TREDWELL, Clerk.

CHURCH AND KING.

Col. Graydon, an American prisoner on parole at Flatbush, got permission to accept an invitation to dine with Mr. Alex. Wallace. He says: "Upon our arrival at Jamaica after putting up our horses at an inn, we took a ramble through the town before we went to our host's. We had strolled to nearly the end of the Main street, when we observed a soldier coming after us. He said Col. Fanning desired to speak with us at his quarters. He wanted to know why we were out of our limits. We replied that we had come to dine with Mr. Wallace who had got permission for us from the Commissary of Prisoners. The Col. thereupon dismissed us. Mr. Wallace entertained us with much hospitality. He put a glass of wine in the hand of his son aged 7 or 8 years, and asked him what he drank? "CHURCH and KING," replied the little fellow. I had contemplated becoming an Episcopalian, yet the boy's sentiment appeared to me selfish and degrading.

SCHOOLS.

In ancient times school houses were built and the masters supported by voluntary contributions of the neighborhood. At the out break of the Revolution probably they were closed. An old lady once told me she was at school when a little girl, and the alarm was sounded: "The red coats are coming, run, youngsters run." That was the last of her going to school. We find the following notice of a school in Jamaica; but there must have been others:

1777, Jan. 13.—Andrew Wilson is now opening a grammar school. Board may be procured at Jamaica.

Simeon Lugrin also taught a school. Nath'l Box, kept school in a sort of a log house at Springfield, near Decker's store.

RECRUITING OFFICES.

As there were many refugees from the Main without employ, recruiting offices were, from time to time, opened in Jamaica.

1777, Sep. 1.—"The people of the little town of Jamaica have contributed £219 to encourage the raising of a New Corps to be commanded by Col. Fanning."

1778, May 2.—"All *Gentlemen Volunteers* who are disposed to serve His Majesty in Capt. Kinlock's Troop of Light Dragoons, are desired to repair to his quarters at Jamaica, where they will find a horse, clothing and accoutrements, and enter on the same pay with British Dragoons."

1779, Nov. 3.—"*Loyal refugees* are now recruiting at Bett's tavern, Jamaica, by Abm. C. Cuyler, who is authorized to raise a battalion of 600 men."

BLACKSMITHS.

1873, June 7.—The partnership between Isaac Roop and Jona. Jones, blacksmiths, is dissolved. The shop, a good stand in the centre of Jamaica town, and one set of tools complete, for sale.

CONFISCATIONS.

The farms of the more active Loyalists in Jamaica were confiscated: Johannes Polhemus' farm of 200 acres was sold for £1,650; George Folliot's farm of 21 acres, sold for £5000; Joseph Ford's lot of 4 acres, sold for £450; George Duncan Ludlow's land, 26 acres, sold for £265.

Some of the Loyalists of Jamaica, at the approach of peace, went into voluntary exile; some to Canada, some to New Brunswick and Nova Scotia. Most of them returned to their former homes after the angry passions of the Whigs had subsided. A few, however, breathed their last in a land of strangers.

It required a great many vessels to transport the exiles. A fleet of 30 vessels, more or less, usually sailed under a convoy, for fear of losing their way. Friends and relatives usually formed themselves into companies and settled together. Here follows an advertisement of a Jamaica Association.

"1783, Sep. 13th. The Royalists enrolled in Capt. John Polhemus' company for Annapolis Royal, are informed that the ship is ready to receive them. The passage will be at the expense of the Crown."

Capt. Polhemus kept a tavern at what is now Woodhaven. When his friends advised him not to go in exile but remain on his farm. He replied, I would rather stay here but I *dare* not run the risk. After some time he, however, found his way back to his old home and died in peace.

It seems by the annexed notice that the slave liked the land of the exile better than his master did:

"*One guinea reward.* Run away from Johannes Polhemus, living at Jamaica, (Jan. 2, 1786), a negro man Brock. He is supposed to be lurking in N. Y. till he can get a passage to Nova Scotia. Masters of vessels are forbid to carry him away."

TRESPASS ACT.

After the British evacuated our Island some of the Whigs sued the Loyalists who had taken their property for the use of the British army. The Legislature had also passed a law that in suits for trespass, no one should plead that he was forced to do it by the order of the enemy. In 1784, May 22, Peter Fredrickson took advantage of this Act, and sued Joseph Oldfield before Benj. Everett, Esq., at Nathaniel Box's inn at Springfield, for taking from him a gun and cutlass, damage £10.

Mr. Oldfield plead that he took them under orders from Lord Cornwallis, that L. I. was then under control of British troops, and that the 6th Article of the Definitive Treaty of peace was a bar. The plea was over-ruled, and verdict given for plaintiff. *A certiorari* was, however, granted June 5th.

Among a great many other suits were:

1785.—John I Skidmore vs. Samuel Simmons.
Abm. Ketteltas vs. Nicholas Ludlum.
Ephraim Baylis vs. same.
Increase Carpenter vs. Stephen Carman.
Abm. Ketteltas vs. Richard Betts.

CELEBRATION OF PEACE.

1783, on Monday, Dec. 8, the glorious event of peace was celebrated at Jamaica by the Whigs of Queens county. At sunrise a volley was fired by Continental Troops stationed in town, and the 13 stripes were displayed on a Liberty Pole which had been erected for the purpose. At 4 o'clock a number of the gentlemen of the county, and officers of the army who were in the neighborhood, sat down to an elegant dinner attended by the music of a most excellent band formerly belonging to the Line of this State. After drinking 13 toasts, the gentlemen marched in column, 13 abreast in procession thro' the village, preceded by the music and saluting the colors as they passed.

In the evening every house in the village and for several miles around was most brilliantly illuminated; and a ball given to the ladies concluded the whole. It was pleasing to view the different expressions of joy and gratitude apparent in every countenance, on the occasion. In short the whole was conducted with the greatest harmony, and gave universal satisfaction. The church bells were rung and there was a free table for the populace. Such Loyalists as were to be found in the streets met with rough handling.

An address to the Governor, Geo. Clinton, was also agreed on.

Gov. Clinton appointed Thursday, Dec. 11th as a Day of Thanksgiving for the establishment of Independance.

GEORGE CLINTON

ranked very high in the affections of our ancestors. He was Governor of this State during the Revolution, and died Vice-President of the United States. He gave $25 toward building the first academy in this village.

He and Washington rode at the head of the army, side by side, into New York when the British evacuated it.

I will finish this narrative with a few lines of an ode on that occasion:

"They come! They come, the heroes come
With rattling fife and thundering drum;
Their ranks advance in bright array,
The heroes of America.

He comes! 'tis mighty *Washington*.
Words fail to tell all he has done;
Our Hero, Guardian, Father, Friend!
His fame can never—never end.

He comes! He comes! 'tis Clinton comes;
Justice her ancient seat resumes;
From shore to shore let shouts resound
For Justice* comes with freedom crowned."

*NOTE.—Our forefathers were anxious to have Courts of Justice re-established speedily, for when the British troops withdrew there was no way for arresting and punishing evil doers. The local militia stood guard over prisoners till order was restored.

REPLY TO MR. COOPER.

GENTLEMEN:—The letter of Mr. Cooper would allow of a wide range of remark, but throwing aside all minor considerations:

The question at issue is—Did Oliver De Lancey, junior, strike General Woodhull, after his surrender?

For the affirmative, we have the declaration of Colonel Troup, who heard the story from Woodhull's own lips, while they were fellow-prisoners. Troup says: "The General told him he was taken by a party of light horse, under Captain Oliver De Lancey; that on being asked by said captain if he would surrender, he replied in the affirmative—provided he would treat him like a gentleman, which Captain De Lancey assured him he would: whereupon the general delivered his sword; and that immediately after, the said Oliver De Lancey, jr., struck him; and others of his party, imitating his example, did cruelly cut and hack him in the manner he then was."

This is clear, definite and positive, and given under the solemnity of an oath.

Troup was a graduate of Columbia College, a Lawyer by profession: of most respectable standing in society, the friend and associate of Jay and Hamilton; a very *conscientious* man, of sterling piety, who afterwards was a Judge, member of our Legislature and warden of Trinity Church.

And yet, Mr. Cooper, by implication, assails the character of such men as Troup and Morris, in order to weaken the force of this deposition.

For the negative, we have:

1st. Mr. Cooper's disbelief that any British officer, and especially De Lancey, would do such an act; because he was born and educated a gentleman, and was a soldier of established reputation,* and that the deed involves treachery, cowardice and barbarity.

To this it may be replied, that Mr. Cooper forgets that the gentler feelings are all stilled in a civil war; and that although De Lancey was a regular, yet he had been so long in this country, and heard so much of the wrongs his connections had suffered, as to have his feelings wrought up to the highest degree of bitterness against the rebels. He had himself been forced to quit Boston in 1776. John De Lancey had, in 1775, been so exasperated at General Scott, a member of the Provincial Congress, as to shake his fist in his face; and again, this John's goods had been distrained for refusing to do military duty. Stephen De Lancey had been sent to Hartford jail. James De Lancey's house in the Bowery had been taken for a rebel hospital; and the mansion of the elder Oliver, at Bloomingdale, was allowed for a like purpose.

Mr. Cooper aggravates the barbarity of the deed, to show its improbability; but let us consider a little.

General Woodhull was president of the convention that had heaped so many wrongs on the De Lancey family, and was the first political officer of note that had fallen in the enemy's hands. What, then, more natural, or probable than that De Lancey should exact a humiliating recantation from him of saying, " God save the king!" and if Woodhull, thinking 'each blow would be the last, preferred hacking to recanting, what mattered it to Oliver?

All historians agree in fixing the act on an *officer*. An old man, aged 85, now living (and who saw Woodhull with his head tied up and his arm bandaged) says " the *officers* did it." If done by an officer, why not De Lancey, rather than Baird, for the above reasons? In Wood's Long Island, page 53, edition of 1824, he says: " Woodhull was suffered by the *officers* to be so cut and mangled, that he died of his wounds a few days after his capture."

2d. The second point for the negative is Mr. Cooper's suddenly revived memory of a long forgotten conversation with a Major De Lancey, in which, referring to this charge of De Lancey's wounding Woodhull, he says, "Oliver always indignantly denied it." If so, why did not Judge Jones say as much? Now, Mr. Cooper's memory, to say the least, is a very convenient one. It recalls to mind, at the precise time of need, just so much as is wanted, without varying over half a dozen words! But does not Mr. Cooper ask too much of us? He should bear in mind that he once gave as authority a conversation wherein it was said, "that the father of Oliver De Lancey died in command, on Long Island, about the middle of the war, and was interred in the family vault in Trinity Church;" an error I exposed by quoting the obituary notice of his death at Beverly, England, in 1785.

3d. When Mr. C. refers to Wood and Thompson, historians of Long Island, as giving an account disagreeing with Colonel Troup's deposition, he is bound to show that they had it before them [which they had not,] and on due examination, rejected it.

4th. But Mr. Cooper's main reliance is on Judge Jones's MS., which is as ambiguous, when Mr. C. mounts the tripod, as ever were the responses of the Delphian oracle. In my letter of May 15th, I pointed out several mis-statements, in order to show that Mr. C. had overrated its value. I will now cite other passages. "The General after his surrender," says the MS., "favored by the darkness of the night, attempted to make his escape; but being discovered by the sentries, while attempting to get over a board fence, he received several strokes from their broadswords, particularly one upon the arm."— The meaning evidently is, that, Woodhull was captured without bodily injury, and put under guard for the night; but taking advantage of the darkness, he attempted to escape, and was wounded by the pursuing sentinels. Now (leaving Troup's deposition out of the question) this is contradicted, by all tradition;

2d, by Wood and Thompson, and 3d, by the testimony of William Warne, a loyalist, who said, while Woodhull was yet living, that he was wounded at Carpenter's, when first made prisoner. Now Judge Jones wrote his history, as Mr. C. thinks, after the war, that is, more than seven years after the event.— What may he not have forgotten in that time? On the other hand, Warne was on the spot, heard his story from the light horse, and told it within a fortnight after, when it was reduced to writing.

All other accounts represent De Lancey as present at the wounding of Woodhull; but if he was wounded when endeavoring to escape, (as the MS. says,) how could he be present? He must have been abed, or at his quarters, and could not have come up with the sentinels at the instant they cut him.

Again, the MS. says—"The light horse were sent to Jamaica the evening after the battle, as an escort to some prisoners taken in the action." Now the action was near Brooklyn, about ten miles west of Jamaica, so that the prisoners, according to the MS. were sent ten miles away from the army, out into an exposed village in the enemy's country, where a hostile force might be momentarily expected; for Col. Livingston was in Suffolk County, marching westward, Majors Brush and Smith also had the militia mustered at Huntington, ready to march. Gov. Trumbull had been requested to send over forces, and the British expected Gen. Lee to land at Hellgate to take them in the rear.— Mr. Cooper, however, interprets the MS. as saying the light horse were sent to escort prisoners (taken in the action) *from* Jamaica. Still, this does not help the difficulty, for if the prisoners taken in the action were at Jamaica, they must have been escorted there. But Troup says, (as is reasonable and natural,) that the prisoners were kept near the main body of the enemy.

That the light horse were sent expressly to capture Woodhull's party,† and prevent his driving off the live stock, which they so much needed, is highly probable in itself, and is confirmed by all tradition. Wm. Howard, aged 85, says: "On the night before the battle, the light horse (who acted as scouts to the enemy,) heard where Woodhull's party lay, and started in quest of him; but on hearing an exaggerated account of his force, they returned." The day after the battle, they set out again, and entered Jamaica village at tea-time, enquiring for Woodhull. They surrounded the house of Robert Hinchman, a noted Whig, who ran out of the back door but was caught and dragged to the front of his house, where he was seen by his daughter, on his knees, imploring mercy with outstretched hands, and the soldiers flourishing their swords over him. Perhaps Judge Jones may have engrafted these circumstances on the story of Woodhull's capture.

The MS. also says, Woodhull was commander-in-chief of *all* the militia of Long Island; whereas his command was limited to Suffolk and Queens.

Judging from the extract, I should suppose

Judge Jones's knowledge of local revolutionary incidents (like Mr. Cooper's), might do very well for fire-side conversation, but is hardly accurate enough, I apprehend, to place him in company with Judge Marshall.

I will now point out a mistake or two of Mr. Cooper's: The battle of the 26th should be 27th. He also says "Oliver De Lancey became major in 1776, and lieutenant-colonel a year or two later;" whereas he was not made major till 1778, nor lieutenant-colonel till 1781.

As many of Mr. Cooper's objections have been met by the restoration of the omitted portions of Troup's affidavit, I will here conclude, hoping Mr. Cooper's avocations will allow him a few moments' leisure to reply to my letter of the 15th ultimo, as I am as anxious to arrive at the truth as Mr. Cooper can possibly be.‡

Very respectfully yours,
HENRY ONDERDONK, Jr.
Jamaica, June 17, 1848.

*Mr Cooper in setting off Delancey's character says: he rose to the rank of Barrack Master General of the British Empire; but he forgets to add that he was deprived of it on a charge of *defalcation*

†The British Military Calender says expressly: The 17th Light Dragoons was detached in pursuit of the American General Woodhull's Corps of Cavalry collected at Jamaica, where Sir William Erskine at the head of the 17th Dragoons and 71st foot, defeated that corps, taking Woodhull and many prisoners.

‡Mr. Cooper has never replied to this letter. H. O. Jr.

OBITUARY.

DIED.—At Manhasset, L. I., 8th of Ferbruary, Joseph Onderdonk, in the 86th year of his age. /852^

He was but little over ten years of age at the time of the Declaration of Independence; a copy of which in the form of a handbill was sent to his father (who was a Whig Committee man) and which he read aloud to his father's family as they were called together for that purpose, after the noontide repast. The events of the Revolution were deeply impressed on his mind. He saw the first movements for organizing whig committees and diffusing whig principles.

After the enemy got possession of the Island, he saw the British Light Horse when they rode up to his father's house and carried him off a prisoner to New York. He also walked amid the ruins of the great fire in New York in 1776 and saw the naked walls of Trinity Church as they stood black and crumbling from the effects of heat. He heard while at work in the cornfield the booming of the cannon at the battle of White Plains. Here collected being in the harvest field in 1778 when his uncle rode in with an "Extra Gazette" containing the news of the battle of Monmouth. In the hard winter of 1780 he saw the British outposts as they were marching thro' the snow knee deep, they having been called in from the east end of Long Island for the defence of New York City whose harbor was for weeks bridged over with ice. At the time Burr's store at Manhasset

Valley was robbed and the owner shot, he was patrolling with a gun, and saw the whaleboats as they quietly dropped down the bay, and he came in contact with one of the crew who escaped with a wound in the chin. He had often to serve as wagoner to the British forces in carting wood and warlike stores, and was once sent with his father's team to transport soldiers' rations from the Dutch church in Jamaica, to Col. Wormb's Quarters at Westbury. At the Evacuation of the Island in 1783, he assisted in removing the baggage of the camp-followers, from Success Church to Newtown. He witnessed the execution at Jamaica of the two men who robbed the house of Thomas Thorne at Manhasset. He used often to repeat in the Dutch language portions of the prayer of the Rev. Mr. Rubell, a Royal Dutch Domine, who in his intercessions never forgot "our good King, George the third, his Queen Charlott, and the Princesses of the Royal family, as well as the Lords of the upper and lower Houses of Parliament."—He also was one of the spectators of the execution of Nathan Hale (who was captured near Huntington) from whose lips he heard a circumstantial account of Hale's last moments. He was present at the Inauguration of Washington as first President of the United States. His experience and observation of British insolence during the armed occupation of Long Island left an impression on his mind which length of years could never obliterate.

At his funeral the Rev. N. E. Smith of Brookville, delivered a very appropriate discourse from Genesis. xxv, 8: "Then Abraham gave up the ghost, and died in a good old age—an old man, and full of years; and was gathered to his people."

Henry Onderdonk, jr.,

Flower Hill School *veiled*

"Dear the school boy spot
We ne'er forget, though there we are forgot."

The origin of this school is ~~vested~~ in the mists of antiquity. In 1721 George Sheresby was schoolmaster on Cow Neck. Rem Remsen, Sr. (who settled here in 1706) had given for the use of a schoolmaster to reside on a lot of 15 square rods adjoining the N. W. corner of Jacobus Hegeman's orchard. On Nov. 1st, 1745, while John Clark was teacher, this site was exchanged for a lot of the "same bigness" on the N. W. corner of Jacobus Hegeman's field, adjoining Andries Onderdonk's S. W. corner, upon the highway. There being no school laws then, the ownership was vested in a voluntary association, whose names were : Benj. Akerly, Oliver Baxter, George Baker, Sr. and Jr., Jos. Baker, Caleb Cornwell, Sr. and Jr., Mary and Sam. Cornell, Sam. Jos., Jer. and Trustem Dodge, Dan. Hegeman, Dan. Jr. and Jos. Kissam, Jos. and Wm. Latham, Joseph Mabbet, Andries Onderdonk, Sr. and Jr., Sam Pearce, John Sands Sr. and Jr., Edward and Sam Sands, Robt. Sutton, Ri. and St. Thorne and John Vanderbilt.

In 1748-9 "Nicholas Barrington was schoolmaster at Flower Hill." He could "teach youth to write the usual hands, arithmetic in both kinds, with the extraction of the roots, as also navigation and merchants' accounts after the Italian manner." Surveying and navigation were well taught then for there were always some boys at school who expected to follow a sea faring life. The teachers were often from the old country and unmarried. They usually boarded round.

They came and went. In April, 1763, Thos. Dodge and Petrus Onderdonk advertise in the N. Y. *Gazette* for a man well qualified to teach a school on Cow Neck, and they say he may be settled with a reasonable support. And again we find another notice in the N. Y. *Mercury* of April, 1773, such as this :

"*Teacher Wanted.*—Any person well qualified to teach school, by being well recommended, may hear of very good encouragement by applying to Andries Hegeman or Daniel Kissam, Cow Neck.

This was for years the only school on the Neck. In 1774 the teacher was Elbert Hegeman, Sr., more familiarly called "Master Elbert." He took the school on his own account keeping a night school also during the winters. His patrons were from 1774 to 1776 and onward :

Thos. Appleby,	John Mitchell,
Benj. Acerly,	Jacob & St. Mott,
John Bashford,	Sam Noe,
Widow Baxter,	Adrian & Peter Onderdonk
Wm Baker,	Joshua Pine
J no Burt's	George Rapelye,
Joshua Cornell,	John & Rl. Sands,
Oba. & Peter Demilt,	Capt. Sandford,
Wm. Doty, weaver,	John Stocker,
Andries Hegeman,	Martin Schenck,
Jona. Hutchings.	Jos. & Tim. Smith,
Abigail Judkins,	John, Benj., Rich., Mary
Jos., Benj , & Dan Kissam Sands,	
Lambert Moore Esq.,	Capts. St. Thorne Sr. & Jr.
Wm. Morrell,	

Master Elbert was probably among the most able faithful, and accomplished teachers. He excelled in figures, surveying, and navigation, so that his scholars came across lots 3 or 4 miles from the Head and Bottom of the Neck, and some took board n the neighborhood.

Among the earlier teachers whose names have escaped oblivion were Master Russel, John Farmer, Jacobus Hegeman. After the Revolution school was kept at Sam. Wood's, east side of the Neck, near the steamboat dock. Here David Underhill, and Simeon Strickland taught. A schoolhouse was also set up down the Neck in the rear of Dan. Bogart's, since Jos. O. Hegeman's homestead, where Miss Searing, Henry Mott, and others taught till it was burnt down about 1810, and the scholars came again to Flower Hill till 1813, when a school district was formed and a house erected on the site of the present Free Church. Its teachers from 1813 to 1835 in succession were: Aaron Simonson, James Gallup, Sands Fish, Norman Smith, D. E. Allen, C. G. Weeks, Israel H. Baxter, Jacob Titus, Horatio Griffin.

About 1779 a schoolhouse was erected in Manhasset Valley on a corner lot opposite Dr. Chas. Mitchell's. Among its teachers were Mr. Proft, Abm. Laton, Jas. Docherty, Arthur Green, Aaron Ely, John Dick, Thos. Rheay, Hugh Lyndon.

At Roslyn the teachers were Owen Ellis, in 1750, James Delianna, in 1796, Jas. Douglas, Sam. Paget, Wm. Fowler, Joshua Smith, Wm. Mitchell.

In 1795 and four years after the State gave some money to the schools; but it was not till 1813 that the school fund was regularly distributed, and North Hempstead divided into eleven districts.

From 1805 to 1857 Elbert Hegeman, Jr., took the school on his own account at $1 and afterwards at $1.25 per quarter of 13 weeks, and a holiday every other Saturday. Same boys paid by the day, Here follow the names of his scholars, five of whom are yet living.

Israel and Violetta Baxter; Geo. Bennett, son of John; Henry, John, and Robert Blades; Henry and Gitty Brinckerhoff, ch. of Abm.; Leonard, Deborah, David, John S. and Jas. R. Burtis; Rich. and Caty Corley, children of Henry; Esther Durling; Thos. Francis; Dan, Geo, W., Mary, Grace Hegeman, Susan and Sam Hutchings, ch. of John; Wm., Martha, Dan. Ireland, ch. of Daniel; Jacob and Elizabeth Jacobs, ch. of Mary; Silvanus Lawrence; Samuel and Wm. Marston, sons of Lawrence; Sam. Miller; Sam L. Mitchell, son of George; Adrian, Geo., Andrew L., Eliz., Peter and Abm. S. Onderdonk; Rem, Minnie S., Cathrina, Dan. and Alletta Rapelye; Wm. and Chas. Ruffle; Augustus C., Matilda Ann and Jos. Sands; Rebecca Schenck from John Mitchell's; Sam. Sopus; Benj. South. son of Ezekiel; John, Phebe and Eliz. Smith ch. of Merrit; Maria Thorne dau. of Sarah; Townsend Valentine; Elbert and Smith Van Cott, ch. of David; Hanka Van Riper, John Watts; Ambrose, Peggy and Maria Weeks, ch. of Daniel; Francis Wright. There were three teachers of the name of Elbert Hegeman.

On Tuesday, April 25, 1809, "Henry began school." So my mother wrote in the almanac. I was probably escorted thither by our mulatto servant girl, Mary Kelley, whose indentures required that she should have schooling sufficient to read her Bible. The building stood on an unshaded lot open to the road and 16 by 13 feet and 9 feet in the stud. It was not painted without nor plastered within. It had four small square windows of nine panes each with shutters. The wide open fire place and chimney on the road side had been taken down and a close iron stove set up in the centre of the room. Still later (say 1813) the house was shingled and painted red, the old back-wall of the fire place taken out and a window inserted so that scholars could see those passing on the road. There was a front and a rear door for ventilation in summer. The room was so open that in winter the large fires charred and sometimes set ablaze the flooring overhead from the heat of the stove pipe. A few cups of water sufficed to stop the burning.

There was a double table of thick chestnut plank much hacked by the knives of mischievous boys. The long benches were of stout, heavy timber hewed and planed. There was a lower bench without a table for the little ones. The girls sat by themselves on the west side of the room. Their seats and table had been newly made of pine. The scholars had to clamber on the seats and desks to hang up their dinner baskets and hats on nails.

There was no outhouse of any kind, and the wood pile was exposed to all weathers. The parents brought wood in proportion to the children they sent. This was cut and split by the larger boys and carried in by the smaller. The first boy who came in the morning kindled the fire from yesterday's embers well covered with ashes in the stove. If, however, the fire had gone out he borrowed a coal from Supervisor Hegeman's.

The larger girls swept the school once a week, and once in a while on Saturday afternoons there was a grand, jolly scrubbing time, the boys fetching water from the Supervisor's pump and the girls brushing the floor with a broom.

There was a pail of water with a tin cup for thirsty scholars. Two boys would fetch water in a pail suspended between them from a stick.

There was no "intermission." A scholar would say: "Master, may I go out?' He then turned a block or tablet that hung at the door, marked "IN", on one side and "OUT" on the other.

Dilworth's spelling book, published in 1740, had given way to Webster; but his arithmetic, published in 1763 still held its ground agaist Daboll, published in 1800. The reading books were the Testament, Bible, Preceptor and Monitor. A sheet or two of foolscap folded once and stitched in a brown paper cover formed our writing book, wherin the master set copies (unless we had copy slips); first straight marks, then pot-hooks, then large letters, then join-hand; and proud were we when we got into fine hand. The master also with a leaden plummet ruled our books and made pens from quills that we brought from home. He stropped his knife on a leather-covered book. A bottle of ink was made from Walkden's ink powder, each writer contributing a cent.

The advanced arithmeticians after showing their sums on the slate to the master set them down in a cyphering book made of a quire or so of paper stitched in a pasteboard cover. Though we had the Rules already printed in the "Assistant," they were copied at length into the cyphering book.

Spelling (out of Webster) was the last exercise every day, and almost the only study that excited ambition and rivalry. The boys and girls stood in long rows, going up and down. The old pronunciation (at least in common conversation) had hardly got out of vogue. We often heard marcy for mercy, vartuous for virtuous, nater for nature, resons for raisins, &c.

Some teachers required the little boys when they came up to say their lessons to make their manners, that is, a small sudden nod or jerk of the head.

The owner of a Dwight's Geography (a reading book) was envied by his less favored schoolmates. Grammar, there was none.

The school went in at 8 in summer and 9 in winter. We had an hour's noon-spell and were let out at 4. We carried in our dinner-baskets a few slices of rye bread and butter with cake or smoked beef, all wrapped up in a white dinner cloth, never sharing our meals with one another. In winter our pockets were well filled with apples.

The earlier teachers used the rod freely, and it was acquiesced in as a matter of course and a necessary means of education; for the dull boy and the bad boy were punished alike. It was truly said of a successful teacher of that day: "He wringeth the boy by the ears and giveth him a strype on the hand with a ferule, he beateth him smartly with a rod. So with sharp correction he giveth him full instruction in the lower sciences." My ears have been soundly boxed for not being able to do my sums.

The teachers up to the time I was kept home to work on the farm were Benj. Sands, Hugh Lyndon, Ezra Lee, and Mr. Griswold. Mr. Sands had the school there three different times. He was a good hearted, worthy man, and unmarried. He used the hickory freely. He would say with grim humor to a delinquent: "Come up here George, and let me take the dust out of your coat." Then he laid the stick across his shoulders. At another time he would call out to Horatio G.: "Look out, General Gates, or Burgoyne will have you." Mr. Sands was partial to pleasant girls, overlooking their faults, readily showing them their lessons, placing a pear on their desks, or challenging them to run a race with him for a paper of raisins. To the less favored he was severe. I have seen four large girls standing up by his desk as a punishment, one of whom he had boxed on the ears. They were all in tears. He also gave the boys pet names. One he called "Jefferson," another "lawyer," another "doctor," &c. He died July 20, 1843, aged 85. *Requiescat in pace.* Amin.

Mr. Lyndon was a good teacher, but in years. He wore corduroy breeches fastened at the knee. He kept blue Monday and seldom staid long in a place. His most angry epithet was, "You consummate villain."

Mr. L e was the first teacher from New England. He required us to call him Mister, and not Master. He introduced new and varied modes of punishment as the ferule, standing on one foot, holding out a stick at arm's length, &c. He set apart Saturday afternoons for speaking single pieces, and dressed the boys in character.

Mr. Griswold taught a night school in 1816-7, each boy bringing his own candle. The scholars being overgrown and disorderly the school was discontinued.

Singing school was sometimes kept here by itinerant masters. The Auroran association of which John Kissam was president and Singleton Mitchell secretary, met here on Saturday evenings from 1800 to 1803. The questions debated were of a practical sort as: "Which is the most profitable, ten acres of wheat, or corn, or grass?" "Is Cow Neck more valuable in its present condition than when it was covered with wood?" "Has music any effect on the mind? If so, what?"

Auroran

When any respectable person rode by us on the road we formed in line and made our obeisance. The civility was usually returned with a smile and some good natured remark. The noon spell was taken up in playing ball, pitching quoits, jumping, hopping, racing, playing horse, "Ispy," "How many miles to Barnabas?" "Puss in the corner," "Here comes a great Lord out of Spain," &c. The girls in ummer often rambled along the hedges for sweet brier, mint, birch bark to chew, &c. Sometimes they had their play-houses and made calls on each other. The boys in winter snow-balled each other, slid on the ice or skated on Minnie Onderdonk's pond. Here Rulef Schenck broke in up to his shoulders, to our great alarm.

Umbrellas were not used. So little fear had the girls of being wet that after a shower they would go in the road and make mud pies. There were few pocket-handkerchiefs, especially among the boys, who wiped on their coat sleeves. Shoes were worn covered with leggins to keep out the snow. One youngster was nick-named "Boots," he being the only boy who wore them.

There was no changing of school books. They descended from the older to the younger till worn out by use. Indeed, books of any kind were so scarce that boys often read the sums in the arithmetic for pastime.

In 1841 the site of the school house was exchanged for the present one, and the old building sold to Charles Baxter.   O.

HENRY ONDERDONK, JR.

Christ Church Academy, Manhasset.

"Those that he loved so long and sees no more,
Loved and still loves (not dead, but gone before),
He gathers round him and revives at will
Scenes of his life that breathe enchantment still."

For years the people of Cow Neck (now Manhasset) and its vicinity who desired a more thorough education for their children than the common schools afforded, were obliged to send them abroad or else have private tutors in their families.

The Rectors of St. George's church, Hempstead, viz: Seabury, Cutting, Moore and Hart had from 1762 to about 1816 kept in succession a classical school and taken in boarders. John Henry Hentz also taught French there; and Rev. Timothy Clowes had an Academy of 60 scholars in 1816 and after. An academy had been opened at Jamaica in 1792, another in Oysterbay in 1802, and Hamilton Hall in Flushing in 1806. Young ladies who wished to learn French, music, drawing, painting, embroidery, &c., were sent to fashionable finishing schools in New York and Brooklyn.

In the spring of 1818 a public meeting was held at Allen's Inn to take into consideration the establishment of an academy nearer home. It was forcibly addressed by Daniel Kissam, Jr.; and after debate a general subscription was started. But at last it was concluded to leave the ownership and management of the Institution in charge of the Vestry of Christ church on whose land it was to be set.

In the fall as I was gathering apples in the orchard, my father came to me and asked if I would like to go to the new academy. I gladly accepted the offer. So on Monday morning, Oct. 26th, we (three brothers) arrayed in our best, wended our way, taking a short cut across lots and along a well-worn path in the Fox Hollow woods, to the much talked of academy, where Lewis S. Hewlett was in waiting with the Principal, who received us bashful and awkward as we felt, with a reassuring courtesy, called us "young gentlemen," and conducted us to our seats.

The Rev. Eli Wheeler had been a tutor in the family of Wynant Van Zandt on Little Neck and married his sister-in-law, Miss Clarina Underhill, (Feb. 6, 1815), and by his influence had become assistant minister of the parish and principal of the academy. He was a good teacher, affable in his hours of ease, smoked his pipe, and was apt to pun on words and chuckle over his witticisms. A parsonage was built for him and he took boarders, some of whom studying for the ministry taught the younger pupils. The clerk's desk was removed from the church into the academy, and in it prayers for a time were read just before the scholars were dismissed for the day.

James Cotter, the classical teacher, had been a "middy" in the British squadron that blockaded our coast in the war of 1812. He was now a candidate for holy orders. He was a faithful but not enlightened instructor, and cultivated the memory rather than the understanding. We learned Murray's abridgement of grammar all through by heart without conceiving what grammar meant. He likewise put us through the parsing exercises by rote, without our having the least idea what parsing was; or did he attempt to explain or in any way illustrate the lesson. So, too, with arithmetic, we were made to commit to memory the rules in Daboll as a task to be learned at home. Accordingly our parents had us up early in the cold winter mornings to con our tasks crouched around the solitary candle on the stand, or crouched in the corner to study by the glimmer of the new-built fire. In reciting our tasks, if a boy missed, the one below who corrected him went up, first giving the delinquent a smart slap on the palm with a thick leather strap which Mr. Cotter kept by him for that use. Cyphering was done on the slate only; as yet there was no blackboard.

Standing up in a long line we read in Murray's Reader, a sentence apiece, going up and down as mistakes in pronunciation and stops were made and corrected. A part of Friday afternoon was set apart for declamation and dialogue. Composition was not so well attended to. Willets' and Cummings' geographies were used. Flint's surveying and Day's algebra were the text books.

The edifice was 24 by 40 feet and 14 feet in the stud. It was surmounted by a belfry (when the bell got cracked a triangle was used), and had two separate entrances in front with lobbies for hats, overcoats, shawls and dinner baskets. The girls sat by themselves on the east side. Their studies were mostly the same as the boys. There was a small room up-stairs (since removed) where the classical scholars might sit by themselves.

Scholars came also from Roslyn, Herricks, Success, Great and Little Neck. Some from a distance rode in winter and stabled their horses near by.

Among the teachers were Mr. Fitch, Harry, Wm. Shelton and Ebnr. Close. Out of school hours they visited among the Priors, Haydocks, Treadwells, Allens, Applebys, Latons, Rapelyes,

Morrells, Mitchells, Thornes, Sells, Sands, Hewletts, &c. Dr. Purdy had added to the North Hempstead Library at the Widow Schenck's books of travel and history, the poems of Youngs, Thomson, Montgomery and Moore, as well as the works of Scott, Irving and Cooper; so that a literary culture was fostered in the neighborhood. The young ladies began to provide themselves with albums in which the gentlemen wrote pieces of poetry and prose, either original or selected. In the Fall of 1823 a Forum was organized with the Rev. D. S. Bogart as president An eloquent opening address was made (Sat. evening, Sep. 6th) by Wm. R. Prince of Flushing, who had a turn for polite learning, and used to write poetry for the *L. I. Farmer* in response to the muse of Miss E. Bogart. The question debated was: "Is duelling justifiable?" Tickets of admission for a gentleman and two ladies, 12½ cents.

In the fall of 1823, having gone over the preparatory studies under Mr. Close, I quit the academy to attend Columbia College. Wm. Robert M. Sands and myself rose at 3 o'clock on an October morning, and Mr. Wheeler took us in his wagon to the Flushing steamboat on which we passed to N. Y. The president frightened us by saying boys were not so well prepared for college in country schools as in the city. However, after four days examination in Greek, Latin, algebra, arithmetic and geography we were called in the chapel on Saturday at candle-light, and our hearts were gladdened at the announcement that we were admitted into the Freshman class.

Mr. Wheeler resigned his situation in the fall of 1823. He had various settlements. At one time he kept a boarding school at the parsonage of Zion church, Little Neck. He died in Brooklyn, March, 1861, at the age of 72.

The Rev. J. P. F. Clarke next had the academy and was Rector of the church from May, 1824, to June, 1832. He tolerated day scholars, but preferred boarders. So the Vestry doubled the size of the parsonage, and Mr. Clarke, at his own cost, added a wing in 1828 for the better accommodation of his 30 boarders, among whom were the sons of Caspar and Hamblin the actors, and D. R. F. Jones, since Senator and Secretary of State. He hired a matron to keep the house in order and look after the boys. Plain as the fare was he always sat on a bare pine bench at the same table with the boys and ate the same bread and drank the same black tea, and if his wife set a nice bit before him he did not touch it. On the Lord's Day the boarders were required

"To be at church and sit with serious looks.
To read their Bibles and their Sunday books."

Mr. Clarke was a classical scholar, theoretical rather than practical; but he solicited advice and accepted suggestions from older and more skilled teachers, as Borland and Forrest in N. Y. He was fond of experimenting but readily modified or abandoned such methods as he found impracticable. He subscribed for the *Journal of Education*, and procured the latest and best editions of school books, and was alive to every improvement; but the day of improved school books and systems of education had as yet hardly dawned. For years the same books had been in use in every school from Brooklyn to Oysterbay. There was no changing of books. Mr. Clarke used Daball's and Colburn's (intellectual) arithmetics, Whelpley's Universal, and Goodrich's and Parley's U. S. histories, and Woodbridge's geography. Walker was the standard of pronuciation. Mr. Clarke distinguished emphatically between Eleizer and Eleazar and pronounced hyssop, hi-sop, and so with oter words.

The first boy caught idling in the morning was mounted on a stool and kept there as a monitor till he espied another idler, whom he called to take his place, and so on during the day. At the dismissal of school the boys had been drilled to march out with a military step. There were two desks on a raised platform at the north end of the room for the teachers, so as to have the oversight of the boys. The girls after a while left school.

Mr. Clarke had hoped to manage the boys by appeals to their ambition or sense of shame, in the use of credit and disgrace marks; but severer punishments came in apace, such as detention after school or on Saturdays, studying lessons standing up, or seated on the "disgrace bench," standing on the floor with extended arm, whipping, and last of all a pair of stocks was erected up stairs under the roof, where delinquents stood solitary with their hands held fast by the wrist in a close fitting opening between two boards. Courts were held on Saturday mornings for the trial and sentence of those who had incurred bad marks during the week.

He issued in 1825 a little twelve-page pamphlet containing a prospectus and the rules of the academy. For board and schooling, $120 and $130 per year, an examination at the close of each term in October and April, to be followed by a vacation of at least one week. The trustees were: Benj. Treadwell, Wm. Mitchell, Lewis S. Hewlett, St. Sell, Benj. Hewlett, Henry Platt, Daniel Kissam, Jr., Thos. C. Thorne, Richard K. Allen, John Sands, John I. Schenck, and Singleton Mitchell.

Mr. Clarke was outspoken and sarcastic. He detested pretence and cant. He was fond of arguing, his opinions always being opposite to those of the person he was conversing with. He did not wish to seem better than he was, and used to speak of Dean Swift having family worship so secretly that a visitor did not know of it. Being asked his age by an inquisitive person, he replied: "Call me 90 if you like." Sick headache was his great trouble. Having found his hearers listless when he preached doctrinal sermons, he became more practical, so that Fred'k Croft, the English teacher, a Unitarian, used to say he had no fault to find with Clarke's sermon's, for

" Averse from aimless theory and strife
He taught the gospel as a rule of life."

Mr. Clarke was very systematic, descending even to the smallest things, as the annexed school bill shows:

      Cow Neck, Jan. 16, 1823.
Mrs. Maria Hegeman,
    To James P. F. Clarke, Dr.
To Andrew James' board, one quarter........$25.00
  do tuition, do 5.00
Ink and quills 6½ cts.; cr. by quills taken
 from him................................. 3½
His assessment for broom and water pail... 3
 do do wood................ 36½
Slate pencil, 1d..................................... 1
A Mentor, 6s; Instructor and spelling
 book, 6s...................................... 1 50
            $31.93½

I was thrice connected with the academy, the last time as a teacher from June, 1827, to Nov., 1828. I called on Mr. Clarke, who said he wished a graduate of Columbia College to relieve him in teaching the languages, and that he would soon be rid of Messrs. Barry and Craft, who could teach English only. I was to have $300 for the first half year and $700 per year thereafter.

Mr. Clarke died Sept. 11, 1876, at Delevan, Wisconsin, where he resided in his son's family.

The Rev. Moses Marcus had the academy in 1836 and Mr. Close and others since. But in course of time the scholars fell away; and carpenters and masons have altered it for a chapel and Sunday school.

Dear old Academy, adieu! In thy hall
Great men have studied while they yet were small.
And scarce was Plato's school in Greece more
 famed
Than thou within North Hempstead's bounds wast
 named.
It grieves me when I say a last farewell
To those old walls that ever pleased me well.

      HENRY ONDERDONK, JR.

Norwalk Gazette.

Tuesday, October 24th, 1876.

New Canaan Fifty-six Years Ago.

RECOLLECTIONS OF HENRY ONDERDONK, JR., NOW OF JAMAICA, L. I.

On the 29th of October, 1821, my father, a farmer, living on Cow Neck, L. I., having heard that 'Squire Eliphalet St. John took boys into his family at $100 per year for board and tuition (and no extras), fitted me out for a six month's stay. He took me, my bedding and a little trunk in his wagon to New York, and left me at lawyer Silliman's, where St. John received his boys, having first bought me a cot and mattress and given me three dollars for six month's pocket money.

Next night at 8 o'clock we went on board the Norwalk packet, Capt. Daskam, and put off from the dock at Peck Slip. I soon turned into my berth, and when I came on deck the next morning, instead of being at Norwalk, found we had run for shelter into Hempstead Harbor, where we rode at anchor all night, the wind being contrary. After breakfast we got under way, and kept beating up the Sound under double reef all day, against a stiff northeaster. So directly ahead was the wind, that on some tacks we made scarcely any headway. The waves ran high, and now and then a heavy sea broke over the gunnels, washing the empty barrels on deck from one side of the deck to the other. The passengers betook themselves to the quarter-deck, where they continued all day long, some lying on their backs deadly sea-sick.

At 4 o'clock in the afternoon we entered still water, running between the rocky islets and trees that studded the mouth of Norwalk river. How tranquil all seemed! How glad we all were! The sea-sick got on their legs again and forgot their late peevishness. We gently glided up the channel, passed the "Old Well," and soon reached the upper landing, where 'Squire St. John's wagon had long been awaiting us. A six miles ride, mostly up hill, took us to our new home, where we were warmly welcomed, and put in good humor by a plentiful supper. We had fasted all day, and some had even thrown their breakfast to the fish.

Next day we were put to our studies. There were half a dozen boarders, and as many day scholars of either sex were allowed to come in. We sat on bare benches. St. John did his teaching himself with the occasional help of his son Lorenzo. His wife had also been a teacher in her youth, and often lent her husband a helping hand. She was strong-minded, read novels as well as religious books, and formed her religious opinions ~~entirely~~ wholly independent of her husband's. He was resigned to the divine decrees, whatever they might be; but she told him she couldn't believe in any doctrines that involved the possibility of her innocent deceased infant daughter being in eternal misery; nor did she begin the observance of her Sabbath till Sunday morning. She was an inveterate snuff-taker. I was left free to advance as fast as my application would carry me, and got on famously with the languages, passing through Ruddiman's Latin grammar, *Historia Sacra* and the third book of Virgil, during the first term.

On Wednesday and Saturday afternoons we had holidays. The boys roamed over the country, while I usually sat alone in the school-room, reading the New York *Spectator* and Norwalk *Gazette*. In summer they went bathing in a stream east of the house, picked blackberries, huckleberries, and in the fall gathered nuts. We passed the winter evenings in the sitting-room, in company with the family.

Our table was spread economically, but always a plenty of good rye bread, large loaves of which were sliced off with a long cutting-knife attached by a hinge to an oak block standing on four legs by the kitchen door. So sweet was this bread that the boys slyly cut off a piece as often as they passed it. Sometimes for dinner we only had hasty pudding with milk or molasses. No butcher ever came near the house; but when fresh meat was wanted the flock was driven from the fields to the barn-yard and the hired man, Mr. Buxton, butchered a sheep.

There was no carpet in the house except in the parlor and best bed-room. Seldom had we knives, plates or table-cloth at supper or breakfast, the bread being ready cut and spread to our hand. We had good appetites and that made up for all. There was no grumbling about our homely fare. On Thanksgiving day the dinner was a surprise. There was no end to the good things; turkeys, chickens, pies, sweet Indian pudding, etc., etc.

The mansion house was double and painted white. It had a stone chimney and stood on high ground, with a row of Lombardy poplars in front. It had a good prospect of my dear Long Island, and oft in the stilly night I stole out of doors to look in silent gaze at the light house on Eaton's Neck.

'Squire St. John had a large farm but being a poor manager, when his purse ran low he took in boarders to recruit his finances a little. Thus he kept school at an interval of every four years. He was taught at Yale

College, and was at first intended for the ministry. He was intelligent, well-esteemed, and had once been made justice of the peace. He had Scott's Bible, Lowe's Encyclopedia, and many other books which I was allowed to rummage.

The observance of the Sabbath commenced on Saturday at sundown, when all had to come in doors, read the Bible, and learn some religious lesson, Sunday schools not having yet been formed there. On Sunday morning all had to go to meeting, and any visitor who staid over Sunday was expected to go along. St. John with his wife, or sometimes myself, rode together in a one-horse chair. A box wagon with bare seats and stiff wooden springs, was filled with boys, and the rest went on foot, it being about two miles. If the pastor was absent a sermon was read by a layman. In returning from meeting the Squire was often in a hurry, and without ceremony would cut ahead of all before him, our vehicle rebounding over the rocks and stones in the road, so that we had to brace ourselves with both hands or else be jolted off the seat.

New Canaan was the stoniest place I had ever seen. The fences were made, many of them, of rocks, and you could walk across many a field without treading on the ground at all, by merely stepping from one stone to another. The red-roofed meeting house stood on high, rocky ground, with no fence around it. There was a gallery on three sides where the singers and young folks sat. On the side hill east of it was an unfenced triangular burying-ground, much neglected. The tomb of Mr. Mitchell, the late pastor, had a railing around it and a tree over it. Here, of a Sunday, I have often seen two aged women with short-gowns and petticoats, with home-made black silk bonnets (not hats) having a cape that fell over their shoulders to keep off the weather. They rode double on a gentle nag, one on a side-saddle, the other on a pillow behind her. As they neared the stone horse-block the animal would sidle up so that they could easily slide off on the block, when they threw the reins over the crotch on the horse-post, shook the dust off, adjusted their dress and then quietly passed into the meetin-house. Considering the roughness of the roads, riding on horse-back was really the easiest way of traveling. When snow was on the ground some used pungs, others put a wagon-box on runners, and a few rode on wheels.

The pews were square boxes with seats on all sides, without cushions or paint. The up-per panel was of open-work. They were re-let every year, which was an occasion of much heart-burning, as one often bid against anoth-er from mere caprice or the fun of the thing. Under the high pulpit was a pew where the two deacons were cooped up. They could not see the minister at all. Sometimes to get a better hearing they rose to their feet and stretched forth their heads a little. An air of mutual acquaintance prevaded the congrega-tion. A Mr. Benedict was so aged and deaf that he was allowed to sit in the white paint-ed pulpit beside the minister. He wore a black skull-cap, and in sermon time stood up with his ear close to the speaker; when he died his son took the father's seat.

There was a stove but no carpet in the meeting house, and no "penny collection" was taken up on the Sabbath day.

There were two services on the Lord's day the year round, with an hour's intermission for noon-spell. Most of the people brought "a bite" from home in their pockets. We had a basket of bread and butter, molasses cake, smoked beef, apples, and the like. The con-gregation were made free at all the neighbor-ing houses, and a drink of water always ready.

We went to Dr. Silliman's and had our provisions spread on the table, and each boy carried his portion. After the people had finished this hasty meal, the more pious got up a prayer meeting which lasted till it was time for afternoon service. When the congregation was dismissed, they did not linger around the house to talk, but hurried off homeward.

The pastor, Rev. Mr. Bonny, wore no clerical robes, but in winter had a cloak. He was courteous, and once told me he should be happy to wait on me at his house. His wife was the real, acting pastor, and by her tact was a help-meet for him. She got up and managed the religious societies of the congregation, and kept things lively. During the week, all the year round; evening meetings were held at the church or in the school houses. When the people were negligent in rising at prayer the deacon would rebuke them, and say: "If they were addressing an earthly potentate would they not stand up? How much more should they do it to the King of Kings." This deacon was the butt of the captious for his alledged short-comings.

The 4th of July, Christmas and New-Years were not observed at all; but on the first Sabbath in January, the pastor gave an account of the church for the past year; how many had died, how many were received in communion, etc. The church bell used to ring at nine o'clock at night all the year round.

Shoemaking was the chief employment of the people. There was a number of free-thinkers who vexed the pious soul of Squire St. John. He listened good-naturedly, and then for the hundredth time answered their objections to the scriptures or their charges against church members. For instance, they objected that Mrs. Judson went about the country soliciting from the poor, contributions for her India mission, wearing a $500 shawl over her shoulders. St. John said "that was a *present* to her from a friend. What would you have her do with it?" Though descended from straight-laced puritans he was no bigot. He once reproved his son for having handed some salt to the hired man on a Saturday night for him to give it to the sheep on the next day. He said that "neither he nor his father before him had ever done a thing of the kind on the Lord's day, nor did his mother make up the bed, nor sweep, nor peel potatoes on the Sabbath." The son asked him: "why he polished his shoes and shaved on Sunday?" He replied: "It should be done on the preceding day, and nothing should be done on the Sabbath but acts of necessity and mercy." The son rejoined: "Our ancestors were too superstitious." The father said: "They had *foibles* but we had *failings*."

Squire St. John once owned a slave, Sib, who had dandled her master when a child on her knee. She scorned to go "to meeting" but asserted her liberty so far as to get confirmed in "the church." The Episcopalians were so few that the Bishop in his visitations was fain to accept the proffered hospitality of some rich Congregationalist. There was no resident clergyman, and services were held about once a month in a forlorn, decayed edifice, a mile or so north of the village. Thither Sib would wend her solitary way of a summer's morning, arrayed in a white dress, with parasol, fan and white handkerchief in her hand. Though bent with years yet at the age of seventy she affected to be but seventeen!

Some slaves from constant attendance on family worship morning and evening, from youth up, had got their master's prayers by heart, and could roll forth high-sounding words with such volubility that you could hardly tell whether it was master or slave that was praying.

A Debating Society met in the school house where metaphysical questions were discussed, such as, "Necessity," "Free-will," &c. One of the school committee, B. St. John, was famed for confounding and puzzling school masters in examining them on the sounds of letters as contained in the preface to Webster's spelling book.

A wagoner (we would call it an "express") passed by our door twice a week, on the days the packets sailed from Norwalk to New York. As postage was then high (twelve and a half cents to Cow Neck) he took my letters to the boat and threw them in the letter-box. The captains, Pennoyer or Daskam, on arriving in New York, left them at Hitchcock's corner grocery, Peck Slip, whence they were taken by the captain of a Cow Bay boat. So round about was the way of letters, but they reached home safely. The post office was kept by a Mr. St. John, in the rear of a beautiful mansion, eight or ten rods from the road. A paved walk ran through the grassy lawn up to the house which was painted yellow.

There was here no free and easy borrowing and lending, as at home. Everything from a horse to a hoe was lent on hire. If a farmer carried anything to or from the landing, for a neighbor, (though it gave him little or no trouble) he expected pay for it.

So deeply was I impressed with my sojourn in New Canaan (1821 to 1823) that I re-visited the scenes of my youth several times in after years. The last time, it was dark when I knocked at the familiar kitchen-door. The old lady with her specs on opened it, holding a candle before her. As soon as she recognized my face, she exclaimed: "Henry! Is it you? Come in." So surprised was she that she forgot she was a widow, and turning around liked to have called out: "St. John! Henry is here."

As I had thoughts of entering Yale College, the following estimate of yearly expenses was made out for my father, by the Rev. Eli Wheeler, 1823:

Board per annum,	$70 00
Tuition,	34 00
Room-rent,	12 00
Wood,	8 00
Washing,	12 00
Use of the Library,	2 50
Incidental expenses, probably,	11 50
	$150 00

BOSTON DAILY ADVERTISER.

FRIDAY MORNING SEPT. 24, 1875.

HALF A CENTURY.

TWENTY-EIGHT HOURS FROM NEW YORK TO BOSTON—STAGE ENTERTAINMENTS—A GLIMPSE OF BOSTON AND CAMBRIDGE IN 1826—A STUDENT'S REMINISCENCES.

[EXTRACTS FROM PRIVATE LETTERS.]

JAMAICA, L. I., Sept., 1875.

Forty-nine years ago (Aug. 24) I left my home on Long Island to enter the University of Cambridge. To gratify the curiosity of friends I left behind, I wrote from time to time some account of my life in Cambridge. As these letters are contemporary, and were written in my boyish days, I have ventured to send them for publication.

Yours, very respectfully,
HENRY ONDERDONK, JR.

CAMBRIDGE, Aug. 29, 1826.

Dear Brother: As I am not yet fairly settled, I should not have written so soon were it not that I supposed you and the rest of my friends must be anxious to hear of me. As you know, the steamboat Washington left New York, 24th instant, at 5:30 o'clock. We had many passengers, among whom was the notorious Colonel Pluck, an ostler elected colonel of a Philadelphia regiment out of ridicule to certain military laws. In the evening, a caucus was held on board, and General Jackson was nominated for President and Colonel Pluck for Vice-President. On the colonel's expressing his determination to stand as candidate he was greeted with reiterated applause. A committee then waited on him, requesting him in the name of the ladies to display his skill in military tactics. Accordingly, in full uniform, that is, with a soiled coat, and cap with half a dozen feathers, white, blue, red and green, spurs (without boots) projecting five inches or more behind his legs, he went through the exercises to the infinite merriment of all assembled. "The bloods" on board were continually amusing themselves at his expense. Though he seemed destitute of sense, yet he made some shrewd remarks. The boat was a first-rate sailer and the accommodations good. As we came near Point Judith it began to rain, and I was prevented from having a good view of the numerous lighthouses and islands.

We left the colonel at Newport, 11 A. M., a showy place of the size of Brooklyn. It lies on a sidehill and rises gracefully from the shore. The wind now became brisk and the sails were hoisted. A gentleman who had a new-fashioned hat like mine lost it overboard. We arrived at Providence 3 P. M., stages waiting for us. Our fare on the boat was $8, and in the stage (40 miles), $3. Had my trunk been a little larger I must have paid for extra baggage. As it rained incessantly the stage-curtains were **down** and I had only occasional views of Providence, but I thought it a very pleasant place. The houses had door-yards with trees, shrubs, vines and flowers, and indicate wealthy occupants who seem fond of comfort rather than making money, which I suppose they cheerfully resign to the New Yorkers. The road was of the first order. We had good stages and rode fast, having four changes of horses. The stage was crowded, the passengers generally moralists. One old gentleman, a farmer, was a Unitarian who, as soon as he found out what I was, said he didn't like "fire and brimstone preaching," that the New Englanders were fond of a cooler climate, &c. We passed through Pawtucket, having perhaps fifty factories. The tomb-stones of the church-yards were, many of them, built of brick 18 inches square, and a flat stone with an inscription placed on top. Though they have had a drought here in the spring the crops are generally good, the fruit not so good. The animated debates that now ensued served to beguile the otherwise tedious ride. A lady asserted that the human race was inferior to the brutes and told of the sagacity of the dog, bee, ant, beaver, &c. An Irishman was much vexed to have "the lords of creation reduced to a level with the brutes." "Self-love" was the next topic, then a denial of "particular providence"—all things being referred to chance. They spoke of the dice-box, drawing-straws, stumbling accidents, &c. A gentleman and lady railed at the Bible as countenancing cruelty and wickedness.

By this time we had entered the public street of the "emporium of learning" and rode two miles in one street. We stopped at the Marlborough Hotel at 10 P.M., 28½ hours from New York. I rose early in the morning. At breakfast I mistook corn-bread for pound-cake, it looked so yellow and rich, and was quite disgusted. The sun appeared for a short time and was succeeded by a drizzling rain of three days. As I had an introductory letter I called on Dr. Ware, who treated me with much civility and took me in his chaise (as it is called here) and showed me many public buildings, the house of Governor Hancock, and the church from whose corner-stone the name of J. Hancock had been effaced by British soldiers; also the Athenæum, a large building with a library, paintings and sculpture. The State house, their noblest building, answers to our city hall. Their mall, or public walk (on which the Bostonians pride themselves) answers to our Battery and is much pleasanter. Their new market is the noblest building of the kind in America. The stalls and cellars rent for $85,000. The old market, Faneuil Hall, still remains. In it were held many patriotic meetings in the days of '76. If you will read Lionel Lincoln you will find much said of Boston in the "times that tried men's souls."

Boston is a place well worth seeing. The houses are entirely different in their appearance from those in New York, many of them having highly ornamented grass plats in front, with trees like those in Sands street, Brooklyn. The city is hilly, the streets narrow and crooked, but clean. As I left Boston for Cambridge by stage at twelve, I arrived at the college at one P. M., three and one-half miles; through a marsh, with sidewalks of planks. The battle ground of Breed's, commonly called Bunker's, hill was pointed out to me. As it was vacation I took lodgings with widow Rogers till the college exercises commence. Cambridge is a dead-level with a few old houses, supported by the students. I called on Dr. Kirkland with my letters. On Tuesday I underwent a most rigid examination by Dr. Popkin, called the ablest Greek scholar in this country, editor of the Collectanea Majora, which his critical acumen and plodding disposition has cleared of many thousand errors. I read with astonishing accuracy nearly all the passages he selected from more than twenty Greek authors—from the Greek testament to Longinus, I was something not far from two hours with him. He made me display all my knowledge of Greek and bid me in translating mention the Greek, and then give the English term corresponding, so as to be certain I knew the individual word. He looked sour at first, but was gentle. My examination in the other departments has been deferred till Friday in consequence of commencement. I am heartily pleased with having come here.

Sincerely yours,
HENRY ONDERDONK, JR.

P. S. Commencement is here a holiday; the banks in Boston closed. The church was filled. The oratory is peculiar. All writing, except of the plainest character, is discountenanced, hence some of the speeches were written in a colloquial or familiar style. At our house there dined some ladies that came out from Boston—all well educated. One read Shakespeare, admired Macbeth," and detected a quotation from "Othello." Another read Virgil, Italian (to go to the opera perhaps when it removes from New York to Boston), and a deal more. She was a poetess, too. Another lady had a sweet voice, and sung with such distinctness that I could understand almost every word. I conversed with an elderly lady (Mrs. Joseph Locke) who told me the Episcopal ministers in the stone chapel were Unitarians.

There were booths for the sale of refreshments around the church. Hundreds were about the tents, all was bustle, drinking, gambling and noise. After the ceremonies were over and the tents were removing, towards dusk I took a walk around and saw several bonfires made. There was much hallooing, dancing and fighting as at our horse races.

On Friday my examination was continued. Professor Otis, a very flowery preacher in the Episcopal church here, opened Cicero de Oratore. I read one passage and he said it was satisfactory. In mathematics I was examined by Mr. Hayward, a tutor, red-haired and freckle-faced. He pronounced me "pretty good." The examination was searching, and was held on two successive days. I now went to Dr. Kirkland. He told me to take a chair in the parlor till he should be at leisure. Directly he came and said, with a smile, if I was master of "Blair" the board voted me accepted without undergoing any further examination.

Your affectionate brother,
HENRY ONDERDONK, JR.

II.

COLLEGE PRAYERS AND COMMONS—CLASS UNIFORMS — SUNDAY EXERCISES — OLD TIME DISSIPATIONS.

CAMBRIDGE, Sept. 14, 1826.

Dear Brother:—I shall now endeavor to give some account of the college. The morning bell rings quarter before six. At six we have prayers. All students who do not attend must, after they miss a certain number of times, give an excuse. A short introductory prayer is made by one of the officers, then a chapter of the Bible is read, and after another prayer of five minutes the students are dismissed. Some then go to a recitation of the lesson they have learnt the previous evening. Some return to their rooms till the breakfast-bell, about seven or after. At eight the study bell rings. All must then go in their rooms and continue there, even if they have no lessons to learn, unless they attend a recitation which occupies an hour. At one, bell for dinner; at two, study bell. At five or after, bell for prayers, and (as the commons hall is under the chapel) take tea as we return from prayers. At eight in the evening study bell. All students out are liable to punishment unless there be a good excuse. Mr. Lunt called me to account for being out as late as nine o'clock on a visit. We have three recitations a day, occupying an hour each. At breakfast we have warm bread and coffee. The table is painted, but has no cloth. We have, of course, plates to lay our bread on. The coffee is not very good, nor the butter. At dinner there is a cloth laid clean every day, two plates, one on another, and a dish of meat. A particular dish and a particular pudding each day. On Saturday, codfish and potatoes prepared in a pan, then rice and molasses for a dessert. When we have cleared the dish of meat we can have no more; but everything else, as bread, butter and potatoes (unpeeled), we have in abundance. Butter is on the table at all times, tho' in small quantities. The servant is often sent from our table for more. Eight or ten sit at each table on benches. There are ten tables in each hall, with one servant to wait on them. Each table has at its extreme two coffee or tea pots, one milk pot and one sugar basin.

There is one advantage—the students can help themselves to as much as they please of anything. Cider and water are placed on the table with a glass for each student. Potatoes are almost the only vegetable sauce we have except when we have beef and cabbage. I have twice tasted squashes, the best I have ever eaten. On some days we have what is called roast pig, tasting pretty well; on some days beefsteak. We have no meat except at dinner; at tea bread and butter. We have the same fare day after day, which makes one a little tired of it. Our puddings are very good—bread-puddings, plum-puddings, Indian-puddings—I mean the *Yankee* Indian-pudding of molasses. The tea, though not unpleasant, has no flavor. Sometimes at tea we have brown bread, made of Indian, and not unlike in color or taste that made of pumpkins. Thus you see anything in the shape of cake is never here. Nor do I regret it; perhaps I should hardly have thought of it were I not writing to you. It is my wish to state all simply as it is. At meals, if the tutor gets in before they commence eating, he asks a blessing; they generally anticipate him, except at tea. Even then they strive to vex him by pouring out their tea, making some noise with the teapot, or turning over as if by accident a bench, while standing, for they rise when he asks the blessing. Few of the officers live in commons. These the students torment while eating, by scolding the servant, setting up a loud laugh and making every noise they can while eating. One can hardly be heard across the table, speaking in his ordinary tone. The one in our hall, who has a very unpleasant countenance and is apt to report students for ill-behavior, is called "Bruin," signifying in English a "bear." The most unpleasant circumstance attending the living in commons is that every one first helps himself and has no concern for another. Thus, those who come late having little left them of what is considered good must take such as they can get. They eat very fast and generally finish in five or eight minutes. I broke off a tooth by hastily biting on a crust of hot bread.

The college halls, four in number, are built of brick, four stories high, without any taste. They have large rooms and can accommodate 200 or more students. A great many board out. University Hall, of white granite, looks pretty well. It has the commons kitchen on the basement floor. Commons Hall is on the second floor, and the chapel on the third floor, or second story. On the next floor above are recitation rooms. The chapel has an organ, under the care of the students, and a gallery for the professors' families. The buildings are nearly all within a stone's throw of the chapel. The professors have beautiful residences at some distance from the college. Some of the tutors live in the college halls with the students, to preserve order and watch over their conduct. The students, though a little mischievous at times, are much more like men than those in New York. It is a maxim that a lie for the benefit of the class is correct,—that is, if it will conceal one from punishment. The students are generally unpopular among the villagers. Every student is obliged to wear a uniform dress as soon after he enters college as possible. This serves to make them known wherever they go, and stops extravagance. Mine cost only $27. The fashion of the coat is singular and strikes the observer at once. Your class is designated by the number of sprigs stitched on the cuff and collar. The caps, too, are the ugliest you ever saw. Imagine a dark mixed-cloth cap fitted to the head and on the top of this a shingle attached one foot square, and covered with the same kind of cloth. The coat is single-breasted with a straight collar. We have services on Sunday twice a day. In the morning the president preaches a practical sermon. He reads his discourses and has little animation. Dr. Ware gives a course of lectures in the afternoon on Natural Religion, etc. There is a gymnasium where the students exercise themselves, walking on a springy pole, or a rope, climbing a rope, swinging and various feats of activity somewhat like those at the circus. This serves to amuse them at recreation hours, when otherwise they might be lounging in bar-rooms, pilfering orchards or vexing the villagers. They have a uniform company and a fire engine.

Our studies are much more laborious than at New York. I am now studying Juvenal in Latin, Hedge's Logic and Farrar's Mechanics; also French. Chemistry is studied pretty extensively. Professor Webster has just published his book, and we attend his lectures in Holden chapel. The library is a sight. It has 30,000 volumes arranged in alcoves. Here I pass a part of Wednesday and Saturday in looking over the huge folios. On commencement day a bar is placed across the alcoves to prevent promenaders from disturbing the books. The names of the donors are written in every book. The names of Hollis and Hancock are painted in gilt letters on a board over the books they have respectively given. There are several full-length portraits in the library of its benefactors; four of them are each ten feet long. There are beside many busts of illustrious men, as Adams, Washington, Hamilton, Wellington, &c. Here are manuscripts ornamented with great care, and a book printed in 1480. The library building is so old that the marble steps are worn down considerably.

The village is two-thirds the size of Jamaica. There is a good deal of travelling through it from Boston into the country, over Cambridge bridge. It has an Episcopal and Congregational church, and three or four stores. A barber, tailor, seamstress, &c, are supported by the students. They have built a theological college here of brick, a very neat building. It is independent of the college. Our rooms are swept by homely old women called "goodies," who also do the chamber-work every morning. Many students have servants to go on errands, clean shoes and fetch water, for the chamber-maids do not put water in the pitchers. The professors sometimes come around the rooms to see that all is well. I have a room to myself,—No. 6, Stoughton, on the second floor, neatly papered,—for which I pay $24 a year. I bought an open stove for $6, a bedstead, a maple table, a looking-glass, a yellow washstand and two chairs—cost of all $18. Some of the richer students have splendid furniture, sofas, large mirrors, secretaries, rich carpets, &c.

Your affectionate brother,

HENRY ONDERDONK, JR.

CAMBRIDGE, Oct. 22, 1826.

Dear Brother: On Tuesday last there was an exhibition in the college, consisting of orations, dialogues, etc., in English, Latin and Greek. The exercises were performed in the chapel, and attended by many ladies. It is a day of general festivity among the students and officers of the college. The speakers generally keep a free table, that is, give an entertainment to their classmates. As most of the speakers were from our class, I had several invitations. In those rooms that I visited the tables groaned under the refreshments and bottles of wine, brandy and punch. Many felt the effects of their revelry. At dinner they did little else than roar and sing obstreperously. The dinner hall was a scene of confusion, noise and good humor. It is the only day when the dishes are not emptied. The wine and cake (the last of which was of the best kind) had completely taken away their appetite. The afternoon was spent in riotous conduct. There is always a tutor in each entry of the students' rooms, who lives there to preserve order; but this day they were at a dinner given by the government of the college, otherwise better behavior would have been observed. These excesses seldom happen. Not more than two students are allowed to stand together in the college yard to talk.

I have been up about an hour. I have a black fellow who makes my fire about five o'clock. I then get up and look over my lesson so as to recite it, which is done as soon as one can see to read. We attend prayers as soon as the president can see to read in a very large print Bible. It is no uncommon thing to see students fall asleep; the seats, being not unlike the pews of a church, are well calculated for it. On September 26th we had finished Hedge's Logic, and were examined on it in presence of a committee. We next took up Paley's Moral Philosophy, reciting ten pages (as near verbatim as possible) at a lesson. Our compositions we hand in to Professor Channing at his study in the rear of his residence, and he makes the merit mark on the margin.

Half-past six A. M. Now the bell is ringing for prayers and I must go. What a scampering there will be among the tardy ones!

Your affectionate brother,
HENRY ONDERDONK, JR.

BOSTON DAILY ADVERTISER.

THURSDAY MORNING, AUG. 24, 1876.

FIFTY YEARS AGO.

REMINISCENCES OF HENRY ONDERDONK, JR., IN CAMBRIDGE AND HANSON.

Today, August 24, 1876, completes a half century since I, a farmer's son, left my home at Flower Hill, Manhasset, L. I., with $90 in my pocket, to enter Harvard College. The cost of passage from New York to Boston was $11 and found. From Boston I rode to Cambridge in Morse's stage, which went twice a day and carried the mail. The fare was twenty-five cents. I was set down at Abel Willard's tavern. My bedding, etc., came by water from New York, and was brought in by John Fairfield, wagoner, No. 17 Central street, Boston. Desirous of knowing something of college life, I took room No. 19, *first floor*, in Stoughton Hall. My classmates (juniors) remonstrated, and said it was a freshman's room, but I persisted in keeping it, amid sundry annoyances, till at last a squib was exploded one night through the keyhole of my door, and then I removed to No. 6 Stoughton. My classmates now called on me, and told me the pet names of the professors and tutors, and the college traditions and stories, some of which no doubt were greatly exaggerated or distorted.

I boarded in commons; Hillard, Norwood, Nichols, &c., were of the mess, though I changed tables once. The talk at our meals was often of our studies, criticisms on the recitations and standing of the students, partiality of the professors, &c. "Why," says one, "there's Richmond, no matter how he recites, Old Hedge will give him 20." Sometimes at dinner one would with his fork stick a slice of meat on the under side of the table, so as to have it to eat at tea-time; and at breakfast take some spoonfuls of sugar out of the cup and wrap it up in paper to sweeten his pudding at dinner. If the doors of the eating-room were not set open punctually at the hour, there was usually good-humored disorder, kicking and thumping at the doors.

Proper decorum was observed in the recitation-rooms, the students hardly whispering to each other. Our class recited in two divisions. Of Paley's Moral Philosophy we recited ten pages early every morning. Wadsworth (since the general), having been up late overnight, was drowsy, but being called up from his snooze by Dr. Hedge (instead of confessing ignorance), endeavored to make up his answers as he went along. The Doctor always required the recitation to be in the author's own words, and W. struggled along till the class got a-tittering, when he dropped down in his seat blushing with confusion. W. roomed at Mr. Danforth's, with Fenton, who acted as a sort of Mentor to him.

The Library

Much of my leisure was passed in the alcoves, to which I had free access. I looked over the titles of the rare folios and got glimpses of knowledge I had never dreamed of. I read the State Trials, Dr. Geddes's Genesis, Bayle's Dictionary, etc., etc. I also took books to my room. The librarian (B. Peirce) had loose paper covers that he put on each book as it was delivered to the student, and took off when the volume was returned. Professors Otis and Popkin roomed in Holworthy. The other professors, who had families, mostly resided in Professors' row and other beautiful places near the college.

SUNDAYS.

Sunday was a quiet day. In the morning we had in the chapel a practical sermon from the president usually, or else from some one he had invited, as Dr. Colman, Dr. Jencks, etc. One Sunday some students, by holding their heads down, seemed to be asleep. Though the president seldom raised his eye from the page, he saw this listlessness, and blushed. During the week these students were called up to state why they had been so inattentive. At two o'clock I sometimes heard the Rev. Mr. Otis, Episcopalian, or Dr. Holmes, Congregationalist. I was startled by a sudden and simultaneous clatter throughout the meeting-house when the people rose at prayer. The pews were unpainted and square, with seats attached to the sides by hinges, and when the supports were pulled away the seats dropped and struck against the side of the pews, and made it more convenient for standing. At four o'clock we had the divinity lecture by Professor Ware. He wore gown and bands, breeches, black stockings and shoes. He had just commenced his four years' course this term, and was now on the threshold; that is, he was showing the grounds on which the Bible rests for its authority, the preferableness of revealed to natural religion and atheism. He displayed much erudition in his discussions. To give an idea of eternity he said: "If you should pick up one grain of sand from this earth at an interval of every thousand years, the earth would be removed in time, but eternity would yet remain; or, if you should take one drop of water from the ocean every thousand years the water would be exhausted in time, but eternity would still remain." To show the absurdity of the world's being made by chance, he said: "You might as easily form the pages of a printed book by the random throw of a handful of type." From the text: "The world by wisdom knew not God," he drew a lively picture of the gross superstition and ignorance of the heathen, who, though well-informed in other respects, yet knew not God. He showed the absurdity of the doctrines of all who did not enjoy the light of Revelation. His discourses were written with great taste, the style easy and his manner dignified, the language beautiful, and he reads slowly, with earnestness and proper emphasis.

At chapel services the marking monitor (Mr. Hale) stood up facing the class and noted absentees. If you came a few minutes after service had begun you were marked "tardy." Twice the students having taken a dislike to the person who prayed, scraped their feet on the floor, making a noise so as nearly to drown his voice. The president afterwards reprimanded them, and made an address on reverencing the house of God.

THANKSGIVING DAY.

On November 30 we had a plentiful dinner of roast turkey, pies, puddings, etc. As I was standing in front of Commons hall Dr. Ware accosted me (to the wonderment of the students) and asked me to take tea at his house that evening. I was there presented to his wife, daughter Elizabeth and his sons Henry and John, with each of whom I had a pleasant talk. The doctor said the first generation of Puritans was more learned than their immediate successors, who had not had equal opportunities of education. He also said that John Quincy Adams thought Locke about as good a text-book to teach from as Reid or Stewart.

There was a seriousness in all Dr. Ware said. He did not indulge in light and trivial talk. His conversation, therefore, was valuable. He gave me advice as to my reading, recommending history and books connected with my studies.

POST-OFFICE, ETC.

Joseph S. Reed kept the post-office. We did not enter the house, but letters and papers were passed through the window to those outside. At night you could read your letters by the light of a candle that stood in the window. After the first rush for letters was over he made out a list of those remaining on a half-sheet of foolscap, which he tacked up beside the window so that he should not be needlessly called out of his back-room where he sat with his family. He could not at first catch my name. "*Huntington*, did you say?" I got the Friday's paper from New York on Tuesday and the Tuesday's paper on Saturday.

On the Common almost every morning in the fall stood farmers in blue frocks with loads of wood for sale, drawn in from the country by a horse and yoke of oxen. Looking across the Common on the west side stood the little village schoolhouse where I have seen of a cool morning before school hours the larger boys chopping and splitting wood and the smaller ones carrying it in for the day's fuel.

Though students were liable to punishment for attending the theatre, yet one rainy night (November 1) a stage was hired and a load of us rode into Boston to hear McCready in Macbeth. I sat next Professor Ticknor, neither knowing the other, as I had left off my uniform. He complained of my elbowing him and I foolishly retorted. For this hardihood I became a short-lived hero among my fellows.

PROFESSOR WEBSTER'S

chemistry was published while we were reciting to him. He had an assistant, but each student in turn was invited to manipulate, or to collect gas in a receiver under water. Their awkward attempts and failures were laughable. The look of Webster's eyes was peculiar, and the picture of his countenance is yet fresher in my mind than that of any other professor. Monsieur Sales was instructor in French. His hair was white with a queue. I bought a Wanostrocht, Nugent and Telemaque. He was out of patience at my inaptitude. I told him I was a Dutchman and my vocal organs were not adapted to pronounce French. This angered him still more.

The students often called on each other. If a tap at the door was not answered the caller passed on without trying the door. I sometimes read Shakespeare with Richmond, each taking a character. I knew of little of any visiting in the village. I had letters and called on Professors Farrar, Hedge, Ware and Willard. The last thought Stewart's Hebrew grammar .. a treasure of learning. With a view of learning Hebrew I had bought Simons's Bible and Lexicon.

SCHOOL-KEEPING.

About the last of November I happened to hear some students talk of going out into the country to keep school. The thought struck me that I would like to see a little of New England life and manners, and also to test my capacity for teaching, so that if I failed my disgrace would not be known to my friends at home. I called on the president for permission. He got the rules, and pointing to "indigent students," asked if I came under that head? I had his consent. In a day or two, Tutor Lunt told me that Dr. Ware had an application from Hanson for a teacher at $16 and board per month. He added that it was a retired place, the people were small farmers, and I would have little or no society there. He gave me a letter to Dr. Kendal at Plymouth, as I would want to see the Rock. Having found Dr. Hodge a good man who had treated me kindly and given me good counsel, I now called on him again for advice in my new calling. He said: "Never turn your back on your school; *obsta principiis*, prevent the opportunity and mischief will seldom happen." I next went to Dr. Ware for final instructions. He sent the following letter to Hanson:—

CAMBRIDGE, Dec. 6, 1823.
To Dr. Calvin Tilden:—

Sir,—I received your letter by mail this morning, requesting me to procure a schoolmaster. I attended immediately to the subject, and am fortunate in being able to procure one who I think will answer your wishes. Mr. Henry Onderdonk, jr., a respectable scholar of the junior class, has engaged to be at Hanson on Friday night, so as to begin his school on Monday following. I suppose this will be sufficiently seasonable notice for you to be ready to have the school opened at that time. I hope and trust that his residence with you will be pleasant to him and useful to those who will be placed under his instruction.

Yours, very respectfully,
HENRY WARE.
HANSON.

On December 7, I left Cambridge for Boston, and found I must take the New Bedford stage. I then went to the barber's, and called on Mrs. Joseph Locke. I slept at Brigham's tavern, arose at six o'clock and went to the stage-house, and waited till seven, then rode about Boston to gather up passengers. I had a cold ride without breakfast. In conversation with the passengers (among whom was Rev. Dr. Dewey) I gathered a few hints on teaching geography by the map without the *definition* of rivers, lakes, etc., and also English grammar by referring to *sensible* objects in teaching nouns, etc. I left the stage at North Bridgewater at 12 o'clock, paid 25 cents for a poor dinner, and gave the tavern-boy a dollar to drive me five miles in a chaise to Hanson. He set me down at Dr. Tilden's. I then went to the door and knocked. It was opened by a good-looking, well-behaved girl with a courtesy. I asked if Dr. Tilden lived here? "Yes, sir, will you walk in?" I followed her, and was helped to a chair, but I preferred standing before the fire. I told her I was sent by Dr. Ware to teach the school. She asked if I had ever taught before? I said "I had assisted in an academy," being ashamed to confess myself a novice. She said "the school was easy to govern," alluding to the disorderly behavior of some schools. I replied: "I had no fear of that," pretending that I was very strict.

From a corner door now entered a little man with a smile on his face, old-fashioned. This was Dr. Tilden. I advanced, gave him my hand and name, which I suppose he did not understand. I asked if he was "Dr. Tilden who had written a letter to Dr. Ware," telling him I was sent by Dr. Ware. After a little conversation I thought of my letter of introduction, and handed it to him. He could not at first make out my name. After reading my letter he appeared more pleased. He asked if I had taken dinner. After some further conversation he proposed our riding to the school agent's. The doctor then put his nag before his well-worn chaise. After enjoying a very interesting ride we stopped at the agent's. His wife, who was busy boiling mince-meat, said "he was gone out." The doctor left me there and went on to visit a patient, and I conversed with the lady, who was a Trinitarian. As we were returning homeward, we met Mr. Bonny, the agent. On being told "this was the schoolmaster," he asked "for how much I was to keep?" He said: "The master must board where he could be boarded cheapest." This I did not like. Dr. Tilden replied that I "should be put in a good and respectable house." We then stopped at the widow Barstow's; her husband, the minister of Hanson, had lately died. The doctor went in without knocking.

We were received by a pert young miss of seventeen (afterwards found her a very good girl), were shown into the keeping-room with a painted floor. "This," the doctor said, "might be my future boarding-house." The doctor asked for her mother and sister. Sarah soon came down stairs. She stooped a little, and wore black buckskin shoes. She was rather pale, and had on a blue bombazette. Jane had on a dark calico, and spoke quick. I was introduced as "the gentleman from Cambridge." The old lady wore a black dress, and appeared rather stern. When asked if she "could board the schoolmaster," she replied that "he had been used to fashionable life and could not take up with their coarse fare." Though embarrassed by her severity, my sense of politeness obliged me to make some complimentary answer. However, after some talking it was agreed that "if the gentleman would take up with their living he might come." N. B. The old lady was on a visit to a neighbor's as I passed by the door, when the hostess said: "Yonder goes Dr. Tilden with his Cambridge fop." The good folks, I believe, really thought me a "Corinthian," for they see little of city fashions. My broad-brimmed beaver, cane, pin, uniform coat, and pantaloons gathered up before so as in appearance to have no falls, must have excited attention. My gold watch, had they seen it, would have added to the rest. The very fact of being a student from Cambridge was enough in itself to raise me in their estimation.

On our return home I was made uneasy by the pains taken to give me tea. Two kinds of cake, two of pie (for they have pies for tea here), to say nothing of other good things. The doctor had a very good collection of books, among them Brewster's Encyclopedia. In the evening I had a spirited discourse with him. I impressed into my service Paley, Locke and Stewart, and discovered here that a little reading will enable one, for a short time at least, to appear learned, for most of what I said was drawn from three months' study at Cambridge. I also spoke of the errors of education. This was to the point. He thought as I did, and told me how he had labored to get scientific teachers in the schools. We talked very briskly till 9 o'clock, when I was shown into a convenient chamber, and what pleased me was a substitute for a washstand on the landing of the staircase. The bed was curtained. Thinking of my novel situation, the difficulty of keeping my school in order and making them learn, so distracted me that I slept very little all night. In the morning I arose somewhat late, had a good breakfast and then the Dr. began on the Trinity and was quite earnest. This talk was partly interrupted by the school-agent, who could find none to take me cheaper than Mrs. Barstow. He was pleased to find me a Trinitarian, but abruptly left us saying: "The Dr. and schoolmaster must visit him and *then* talk it over."

The Dr. took me before dinner to the widow's, saying, "If I was not pleased with the family he would be mistaken." I replied; "So would I." He then carried my trunk in and I followed. As it was near noon I stood up by the fire and conversed freely with the family. Perhaps I was rather pedantic, for when a plate split in two by the too sudden application of heat I showed the cause, referring it to chemical agency, and recommended the study of chemistry. Our dinner of codfish, boiled simply, potatoes and a gravy made by frying pork cut in strips, with brown Indian bread (the usual Saturday's dinner), was rather forbidding, but I yielded to circumstances and ate with a good grace. An apple-pie concluded our homely fare. This became to me a very good dinner ever after. To show my condescension I put shingle panes in the kitchen windows. I next took a view of my schoolhouse, which I found very open, old and poor, like many on Long Island. It was not painted; a fire-place was at one end, with an entry on one side and wood-closet on the other. The tables stood on three sides of the room, and the girls had to step on them to hang up their bonnets, shawls and dinner-baskets. There were rude benches, without backs, for the smaller children, in the middle of the room. On my return Sarah told me that she had taught in the summer, and I asked her the mode of teaching and talked over school affairs generally. Without her advice I should have had poor success. I borrowed her copy-slips; quills were in use, and I was an adept at pen-making.

The school, which I supposed was less than thirty, I now found would exceed forty. I slept very little this and the next night from the school-fear. Before retiring I had a piece of cake—the same kind that was on the tea-table. By the way, our tea was more to my notion than the dinner. We had black tea and good plum-cake. I had a large, airy bedroom alone; a brass warming-pan had been passed through the sheets to take off the chill. The girls' dresses hung up in the room. The books on the mantel-piece were Leslie's Review of the Deists and Morse's Geography. There was a table with a white cover and looking-glass, but no wash-stand, the morning's ablution being done in the kitchen. Our breakfast was of rye-coffee, rye-cakes fresh baked in a pan, and meat —all very good. The brown bread was excellent also. On Sunday morning we read a chapter in the Testament as an act of devotion. I did not go to meeting, but on asking Jane for "the text" she could not tell. It was a question my father always asked of me. In the evening a wood-fire was kindled in the parlor, the floor of which was painted in fancy patterns, and Sarah introduced me to two of the beaux.

On Monday morning, with troubled mind I went to the school. Dr. Tilden having marshalled the scholars they rose to honor my entrance. I appeared as large as I could, and conversed a little with the doctor. When he left I made an off-hand address to the scholars and took down their names, which, as they were very long, was troublesome. (This list I yet have.) I then heard them read. I was much confused. They could not understand my high-flown language. As I knew not the names of the scholars I could call them to me only by signs, and these they would not understand. The uncouthness of some of the children also surprised me. So ill-bred were they that they would not answer me politely, but made an ignorant stare or insignificant grin. Thus was I, a scholar of Harvard College, in the district school of Hanson. Sarah felt sorry for me, and thought I had no idea of the kind of school I was to take, and that I would soon leave. But I continued and was commended as a teacher; the rough edge of the children's manners grew smoother, and we got along very pleasantly together on the whole. Some apprentice boys had boasted that they would not let the master flog them, whereupon Dr. Tilden came in school and said if any boy resisted the teacher the trustees would come in and inflict corporal punishment. There were boys large enough to have pitched me out of the window, but these were the most orderly of all.

Puzzling questions and hard sums were sent in to me by those who wish to sound the teacher's depth. Drs. Ware and Hedge had forgot to caution me against these intermeddlers, so I accepted the questions in good faith. Some I solved, others I did not.

The society in Hanson was sufficiently pleasant. Seldom was an evening's conversation carried on without some religious argument. Twenty years before the people, except two or three, were of one belief. Afterwards a few became Baptists, some Arminians and then Unitarians. The church was now thinly attended; the pastor, the Rev. P. Howland, was a Hopkinsian.

I called, by invitation, on Mr. Barker. He lent me Ballou's book on Universalism. He had soup and pork for dinner. Not being used to fat salt pork I swallowed the slices whole without chewing. I also, on an evening, played cards with the ladies at Dr. Hitchcock's. The doctor could not pronounce my name, so he got a piece of chalk and had it written on the top of the Franklin stove so that he might spell it out. He was an army surgeon in the Revolution. He said (on learning that I was Dutch) that he once on a Sunday morning stopped at a tavern in Jersey, and there was a crowd of people within and without. Returning in the afternoon he called at the same tavern, and all was lonesome. On inquiry the landlord said the crowd he saw was the Dutch congregation, who had now gone home. I felt ashamed that the Dutch had such a reputation, but I felt his description must be true from what I know of the drinking habits on Long Island before and after church services on the Lord's day. On leaving school it was with regret that I parted with the amiable family where I had passed so many happy hours. I gave souvenirs to the daughters and my room furniture at Cambridge to the mother as a recognition of their kindness. My success in teaching at Hanson determined my future vocation in life.

On leaving Hanson I called on Rev. Mr. Allen of Pembroke, who also carried on farming to eke out a livelihood. He took me on Sunday evening to a wedding. The couple to be married stood up alone. He read a certificate from the justice of the peace, made a few remarks, the parties closed and loosed hands, and a prayer closed the simple ceremony. We then had the usual entertainment. We had so free and easy a conversation that on my taking leave he playfully forgot my name and said: "Mr. Orthodox, when you come this way again I shall be glad to see you."

MY COLLEGE TERM BILL FROM SEPTEMBER 1 TO DECEMBER 20, 1826.

Steward & commons	$3 50
Board in commons	21 25
Rent of room	8 00
Care of room	2 20
Instruction	26 00
Use of library	1 00
Books bought	4 15
Lectures	1 00
Fire-wood	5 40
Catalogue, commencement dinner, etc	60
Repairs	1 07
Total	$71 26

*The Dr. said the school committee would not examine me, for being a college student I was *ipso facto* qualified; but he handed me this paper:—

HANSON, Dec. 9, 1826.

This certifies that the school committee of Hanson having satisfied themselves respecting the literary qualifications of Mr. Henry Onderdonk, jr., do appoint him as a teacher of one of the public schools in said town.

Per order,
CALVIN TILDEN,
For and in behalf of the committee.

THE GREAT DAY.

The Nation's Centennial Anniversary and Its Observance in Jamaica

Jamaica Gay in Bunting and Fireworks—
The Public School Flag Raising and the
Programme of Exercises at the Town Hall—
Henry Onderdonk's Historical Reminiscences for Everybody to Read—The Celebration Elsewhere.

The night of the third of July saw the beginning of the deafening noise that was to be expected on the Fourth, and it was continued through the night. The firemen had taken extra precaution to guard against the destruction of property by having their machines equipped so that horses could be attached, and men had been detailed to duty with military discipline. It was only natural that they should make all the noise possible, and when the meandering youth with guns, pistols and small cannon added their thunder to that of the horse fiddles and fish horns, it became a pondemonium that murdered sleep and called forth the execrations of the less patriotic and sluggish.

THE BEAUTIFUL DAWN

of morning left no doubt that 'old Sol would scorch and burn with a fierceness equal to the few preceding days, and made those who loved quiet and comfort betake themselves to other regions. Rockaway was the favored place. Still, enough remained at home to make the celebration interesting, and there was no apparent diminution of interest, or "cessation of hostilities" by Young America. The cannon for which the Committee paid $60 was about equal to one or two owned in the village which could have been had for the asking; but as it was only auxilliary no particular interest was taken in it, and it could well have been dispensed with.

THE FIRST OF THE EXERCISES.

It had been arranged that the new flag for the school building should be raised at half-past eight. The attendance was quite large, but the exercises by the school did not justify the previous announcement. Very few of the children took part, and the singing was weak and uninspiring. Miss Addie Pearsall raised the flag, and Lewis L. Fosdick, Esq., delivered a very appropriate address—liberal in its conception, patriotic, and imbued with commendable public spirit. "Let criticism be full and free, but let it be fair," said Mr. Fosdick, and every liberal mind will say Amen!

THE PROGRAMME AT THE HALL.

At ten o'clock the large room of the Town Hall was three-fourths full. Rev. J. V. Saunders made the opening prayer, Miss Holland read the Declaration of Independence, and John J. Armstrong delivered the oration. Mr. Treadwell read his original ode, composed especially for the occasion:

THE CENTENNIAL ODE.

From each mountain's granite peak,
Where the eagles refuge seek;
From each hillside, from each plain,
Where is heard the shepherds' strain;
From the city's strife and din,
With its wickedness and sin;
From each hamlet, village, town,
From each farmhouse old and brown;
From our whole united land,
To its uttermost expand,
  Let the shout
From the hearts of all ring out,
That a nation glad and free
Celebrates its jubilee.

Free from Maine's untrodden snows,
To where the Rio Grande flows;
Free from the Atlantic's waves,
To the coast Pacific laves;
Free in fact as well as name,
Write it on the scroll of fame,
Read it, all ye nations round,
Read it ye who've long been bound,
Read it writ by truth's own might,
Every man shall have his right,
  Worth alone,
Based on merit we enthrone,
And invite the world to see,
Freedom's own prosperity.

We have maidens bright and fair,
Pure as white winged seraphs are,
We have men as bold and brave
As e'er fought their land to save,
We have manhood in its prime,
Youth to guard our future time,
Age its wisdom to impart,
Freedom's home to cheer the heart,
By the present and the past
We will swear that to the last.
   We'll defend
Freedom's birthright to the end;
For her glories take our stand
And protect our native land.

God and country be our boast,
'Mid life's changes uppermost,
Scions of a noble stock,
Sons of men, of Plymouth rock,
Sons, whose fathers side by side,
Fought in Freedoms cause and died;
Men above ignoble tricks,
Martyr men of sev'uty-six,
Let us worthily engage,
Pure to keep our heritage.
   Worthy prove
To the names we honor, love,
Cherished, for our nation's worth ,
Through their death throes wrought its birth.

   One hundred years!
   What hopes, what fears,
   What joys, what tears,
   What progress made,
   What error stayed,
   What might displayed.
Where once a wilderness appeared,
Where once the savage foe was feared,
Where scarce a white man's foot had trod,
Or ploughshare turned the pristine sod;
Where o'er a vast and wide domain,
The savage and wild beast held reign,
Now city, town and hamlet stand,
While all about, on every hand,
Prosperity has blest our land.
   Titanic power,
   Crowns every hour.
   On every hand,
   The triumphs grand,
   Of honest toil we see.
   Millions of hands,
   Like iron bands
   Hold in their grasp,
   With firmest clasp,
   The fruits of industry.
From Maine unto the Golden Gate,
From Oregon to Southmost State,
Each mighty river, lake and stream,
With trafic's busy minions team;
From valley, plain, and mountain gorge,
The smoke of furnace, noise of forge;
The mingled hum of busy wheels,
The magic pulse of commerce feels.
   The giant steam,
   Like fabled dream,
   Wakes into life,
   To aid the strife.
The iron steed its master knows,
Harnessed by science 'gainst its foes,

On beds of steel, with mighty power,
Dashing at fifty miles an hour,
   Ploughing the sea,
   Relentlessly,
   Throwing the spray,
   As if in play,
The proud ship starts from home away.
   Magnetic wire,
   With tongue of fire,
   Man's wants make known,
   From farthest zone,
Along the ocean's briny bed,
With miles of glinting spray o'erhead;
Through forest deep and mountain glen,
O'er prairie vast, where e'er hath been,
The foot of man, there science rears
Her trophies, crowning all the years,
Progress appears on every hand,
Ours is a most progressive land.
The lad of "sev'nty-six" knows more
Of science, than the *man* of yore;
Each college and academy,
A bulwark is of liberty;
And knowledge helps in every state,
Our freedom to perpetuate.
Our laws have opened wide the door,
Knowledge is free to rich and poor;
No law of caste or irksome rules,
God bless the nation's common schools.
   Our church and State
   Are separate,
   While conscience free,
   We worship Thee,
Great source of all divinity.
Dark were the days at freedom's birth,
'Tho hope had not forsook the earth;
Sturdy men were the men of yore,
Hearts of oak in their bosoms bore.
   Many a name,
   Now dear to fame,
From out the gloom and darkness came.
   And freedom's throes
   Were fraught with woes,
For hers were most relentless foes.
They could hear the reveille call to arms,
It was answered from workshops, schools and farms;
All over the land the patriot cry
Was *fight for your freedom, conquer or die* ;
Liberty's boon must be fought for if won,
Mother and daughter urged father and son;
The trusty musket was shouldered with pride,
As a tyrant's wrath bold freemen defied.
Untrained and unskilled in the arts of war,
But fired with a zeal that was better far,
It mattered but little what did oppose,
They were more than a match for British foes.
They knew not of fear, its meaning or name,
But marched to the front as brave Putnam came,
His plough in the furrow left standing still,
While he grasped his gun with an iron will.

   Brave as the men of Bunker Hill,
   Like statues standing grim and still,
   'Till Prescott's sword was seen to rise,
   As shown the whites of British eyes;
   Twice the enemy charged the hill,
   "Fire low" was Prescott's order still,
   'Till powder gone, each ball of lead
   Lodged in a British "red coat's" head.

We've raised a monument to tell
Where patriots with brave Warren fell;
And as the years roll on we still
Shall speak with pride of Bunker Hill.
 For seven years
 With groans and tears,
Baffled by hope, alarmed with fears.
 They struggled on
 Till all was done,
And vict'ry crowned what valor won.

We are standing in our pride on the pinnacle of years,
In looking back we see the flood of human joys and tears ;
We see the triumph of our race in true enlightenment,
The havoc made by fire and sword, the blood and treasure spent.
The altar fires by freedom built a hundred years ago,
That all along the century have shown with steady glow;
We see the heroes of the past rise up in grand array,
Their deeds heroic form a part of history to day ;
Brave Ethan Allen's words ring out, we hear them once again,
As clear as when at early morn they rang o'er Lake Champlain ;
And Sergeant Jasper's bravery we never shall forget;
Look! see him nail the battle flag to Moultrie's parapet;
Hear brave old Stark at Bennington, say just before the fray,
List! "Molly Stark's a widow, boys," unless we win to-day;
A thousand Hessians bit the dust, or flew in mad affright,
The boys of Bennington had won a battle for the right.
Ten thousand guineas England's King had offered General Reed,
To desert his country's cause in her sorest hour of need ;
Brave was his answer, "I am not worth purchasing," said he,
But England could not even buy so poor a man as me.
The Winter spent at Valley Forge, our country's darkest night,
To many hearts it seemed that Fate, fair freedom's cause would blight;
But 'mid those trying scenes appeared the guiding hand of one,
The Israelites their Moses had, *we had* our WASHINGTON!

We stand upon the threshold of another century,
But no plummet can determine its depth of mystery;
We are ages in advance of a hundred years ago,
And who can tell the progress the next century will show:
The discoveries of science, developments of art,
Unravelling of mysteries that now we know in part ;
The wonders of philosophy yet feebly understood,
The links to forge to bind mankind in common brotherhood ;
Relations that our system bears to all the starry spheres;
The changes in the heavens, through the many cycling years;
The wonders that are hid beneath our planets crumbling crust,
The origin of things that erst have been resolved to dust,
Relation matter bears to mind in all its mystery ;
Bringing to light antiquities and treasures of the sea;
Where instinct ends and reason dawns in man, or bird, or brute ;
What causes seed to germinate or tender shrub to shoot.

Great God, before Thy searching eye,
All darkness fades, all shadows fly,
On Thee alone we may rely,
And Thou alone canst satisfy.
Unveil the brightness of Thy face,
That shadow may to light give place,
And man inspired by God shall see,
What now is wrapped in mystery.

Our country, land of all the earth, the one to us most fair,
Where rich and poor, and high and low, breathe freedom's holy air;
Where the poor man is the peer of the wealthiest in the land,
And the only test demanded is an honest heart and hand
May thy banner always wave in its majesty and might,
The exemplar of true freedom and symbol true of right,
That the nations from afar, as they gaze from o'er the sea
May honor thee, *Columbia*, land of the brave and free.

Rev. Dr. Van Slyke followed in a brief address, which was well timed, and fitly chosen. Henry Onderdonk, Jr., Esq., was then introduced. It was his allotted part to read an historical essay of the men and action of Jamaica a hundred years ago; the part her sons took in the war for independence, and the revolutionary incidents connected with Jamaica. Mr. Onderdonk had but just entered on the most interesting part of the narrative, when the bells began to ring, and Mr. Ballard, without any apology to Mr. Onderdonk or the audience, announced that the exercises would close with the singing of the "Star Spangled Banner." The historical address was regarded as the most interesting feature of the day's exercises, and the abrupt and ungentlemanly manner in which it was eliminated caused just and general indignation. There is a very general demand for the publication of the address, and we cheerfully comply, giving so much thereof as space will permit in this issue, hoping to conclude it in our next.

Illuminations and Decorations on the 4th.

IN JAMAICA.

At the residence of Col. Aaron A. Degrauw, President of the village, there was a display of fire-works—rockets, fireballs, colored lights, fire-balloons, etc. The spacious grounds in front were tastefully decorated with flags, colored lanterns, and other designs; the lanterns hanging in grouds and festooned under the trees so that the general effect was very beautiful. The front of the house was also tastefully decorated with flags and lanterns. There was a large company of ladies and gentlemen assembled, and the lavish hospitality of the Colonel and his family was much enjoyed. An incident of the evening here was a visit of the "fire laddies" who were handsomely entertained and who left with "Three cheers for President Degrauw and his wife."

The decorations at the residence of Geo. H. Creed were tastefully arranged, and showed good judgment in the matter of arrangement and selection of articles used for the occasion. Mr. Creed had the largest American flag floating, in the village.

Mr. Abm. L. Bogart's residence presented a very neat and acceptable appearance. If the Union colors ever showed to good advantage they did then and there. Illuminated in the evening.

Stehlin's segar store, and Barget's drug store looked nice, and were tastefully arrayed in flags and evergreens.

Peck's Hall of Pharmacy attracted much attention. The decorations were elaborate and handsome. In one of the large front windows were tasteful transparent paper figures, 1776, and in the other 1876. Flags covered the building from roof to sidewalk a large circle of flags with an eagle in the centre, swung in the doorway. At night all the front windows in the building were illuminated with a candle in every pane of glass, relieved by two small flags triangulated, and colored lanterns swayed across the front.

Benj. W. Vandervoort decorated the Post Office window in a neat and tasty manner, and when illuminated in the evening, had a pleasing effect. B. Faber, next door, shoe store made a grand display of flags and illuminations in his window.

The decorations at the rooms of the Rod and Rifle Association, both inside and out, elicited the praise of all observers. At night the illumination was very attractive and handsome. Much to the disappointment of the Association and the public, a large number of whom had assembled, patiently waiting for the "band to play," the musicians failed to put in an appearance.

Centennial Hall, on Washington st., as well as the dwellings of Messrs. Joseph B. and John Everitt were elegantly decorated; the Hall was a beautiful sight, viewed from any point, bedecked with flags of all nations while high above all, proudly floated the stars and stripes from the staffs on either end of the building.

Mr. Charles H. Huntting made a grand display of flags, both outside and inside of his dwelling. Illuminated in the evening.

The following list comprises some of the most prominent decorations of the day:

On Fulton st., George Snary, ex-Sheriff Durland, J. D. Kolyer, Mrs. Spillett, Jacob Gius, Geo. M. Bennett, Nostrand & Remsen Mr. Marten, Richard Brush, James T. Lewis, Elijah Raynor, Thos. W. Clary, John D Brinckerhoff, Edwards Bros., Geo. E. Tilly Nathan Cohen, Jos. Bernhard, E. W. Halsey "Fulton club," Paul Barthol, Brush's Co tral market, Dr. S. Hendrickson, Hon. Moris Fosdick, Ephraim Baylis, John Weis. Smith B. Crossman, Conklin's Photo Gallery, Jas. A. Fleury, Philip Hardenbrook Mrs. John M. Johnson, Mrs. S. L. Spader, John H. Sutphin, Benj. E. Vandervoort, Ezra W. Conklin, Abm. H. Remsen, John Hirst, Frank G. Crossman, Mrs. S. J. Young George W. Damon, Thomas J. Wayne and Richard Busteed.

On Canal st., Foster B. Hendrickson, L. M. Jaggar, Amos Denton.

On Puntine st., Charles Welling, Wm. L. Denton, Mrs. Orchard.

Abram DeBevoise, and Joseph Ashmead, on North st., made a very attractive display of flags, bunting and colored lanterns.

On Clinton ave., Dr. Beldin, Geo. Skidmore, Col. Wm. Cogswell, Theo. J. Cogswell, Rev. G. Williamson Smith, Peter W. Remsen.

On Union ave., Stephen Shannon, Augustus Treadwell, C. H. Harris, B. F. Hewtetl, Mrs. G. S. Bennett, Hendrick Lott, Prot. Eng. Co. No. 1, Hook and Ladder Co. No. 1, Richard Rhodes, John C. Acker.

On Herriman ave., Mrs. M. L. McCormick, A. Dunham, Samuel S. Aymar, Benj. Robertson, Wm. Shaw, Lewis L. Fosdick, Benj. J. Brenton.

Union Hall st., Hon. Alexander Hagner, J. B. Robertson, Mrs. Shelton, Jos. Bowden, C. J. Stewart, John M. Crane.

We have endeavored to name all who decorated or illuminated on that occasion; if we have omitted any name it is an oversight.

The St. Joseph's Brotherhood had a picnic on Prospect Lawn. There was a very large assemblage who had a good time.

The Capture of Fort St. George, at Mastic, on the South Side of Long Island.

BY COL. TALLMADGE, NOV. 22, 1780.

During the Revolutionary war the British had possession of Long Island; and their adherents occupied the houses and lands of the Whigs who fled from their homes. Among the refugee Whigs from Suffolk county was Gen. John Smith, whose possessions covered several thousand acres of woodland now in tenure of E. Tanjore Smith.

Having heard that the enemy were cutting off immense quantities of his wood and sending it to the New York market where it sold for a high price, Smith applied to Gen. Washington for a force to be sent over to dislodge these depredators who had erected a substantial Fort and a picketed enclosure for their defence.

Col. Tallmadge was entrusted with the management of a secret expedtion for this purpose. He crossed the sound with 80 men, hid his boats in the bushes by the water side and marched by night across the Island, from Old Mans to Mastic. On his route he called at a house where Mrs. Smith was staying after having been driven from her own by the loyalists, told her his destination, and expressed an apprehension that in the conflict he might be compelled to destroy her house which the loyalists had embraced within their Fort.— "Destroy it and welcome, if you can drive out those Tories," replied this patriotic dame.

Tallmadge now took Wm. Booth for a guide and as he neared the sentry of the Fort, he crept along the ground, and watched till his back was turned when he rushed on and the sentinel was dead before he knew whence the bayonet thrust came.

The Fort was at once invested and the watch-word "Washington and Glory" was shouted forth simultaneously on the three sides, as the victors cut down the pickets and rushed into the centre of the parade. Thus was the Fort taken by surprise and almost without a blow. As the victors stood elated with joy a volley of musketry was discharged on them from the 2nd story of Mr. Smith's house, which formed a corner of the stockade. In an instant the doors were broken in by the enraged Americans who darted up stairs and pitched all the men they could lay hands on out of the windows—they having forfeited their lives, by the rules of war. All would have been massacred on the spot had not Col. Tallmadge humanely interfered and stopt the carnage. In 10 minutes all was quiet again.

It was now sunrise, and never did Sun rise more pleasantly to exulting captors. Having secured their prisoners, demolished the fort, burnt the vessels at the dock, and destroyed an immense quantity of goods, they set out on their return, and as if this were not glory enough for one day Col. Tallmadge, on his way back, detached a party to Corum, who burnt an immense quantity of hay stacks (300 ton), intended for the British Cavalry in New York City.

There was no exploit of partisan warfare during the whole Revolution that exceeded this. Col. Tallmadge in 21 hours marched 40 miles, captured a Fort, destroyed all the military stores, burnt 300 tons of forage, and carried off upwards of 50 prisoners; and all this without the loss of a single man! We need not wonder that he received the particular commendation of Washington.

The vestiges of the old Fort are still to be seen at Smith's Point, Mastic, where the writer hereof was shown and told many things that have never yet found their way into history. The Col. committed the preceding plan and sketch to paper for the benefit of his children who now possess the manuscript.

Fort St. George was 96 feet square, and as will be seen by the above cut, was connected by a strong stockade with General Smith's Mansion and a smaller house. These were both barricaded, and from the larger house, it was, that the Tories fired on Col. Tallmadge after the capture of the Fort. The dotted line denotes the passage Col. Tallmadge through the pickets and onto the main Fort.

HENRY ONDERDONK, JR.

ATTACK ON LLOYD'S NECK.

July 12th, 1781.

LONG ISLAND'S CONTRIBUTION TO THE CENTENNIAL, BY HENRY ONDERDONK, JR.

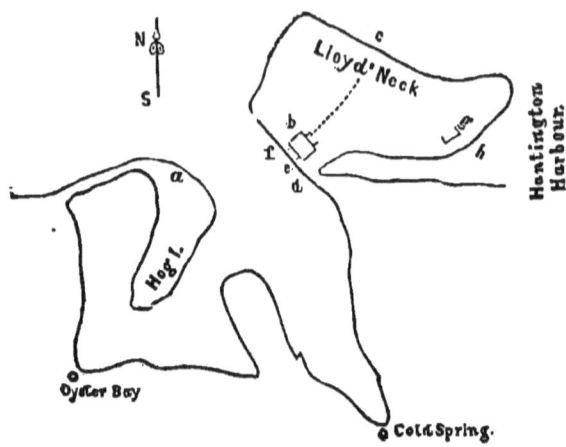

The repulse of the combined French and American forces at Lloyd's Neck, July 12th, 1781.—*Narative of a spectator of the conflict.*

During the Revolutionary war the British took possession of Lloyd's Neck, and erected a small Fort there for the protection of woodcutters, who were mostly refugees from New England. Lloyd's Neck, at that time, was covered with the finest and largest growth of timber imaginable, some trees growing to the height of 40 or 50 feet before a single branch put forth. The refugees gained a livelihood for themselves and their families by cutting down these noble trees for firewood, and sending it to New York, where fuel was in great demand for the use of the King's army cantoned there during the idle hours of winter.

The Americans had made sundry predatorial attacks on this peninsula by night, and carried off some property and prisoners, but on the arrival of the French fleet at Newport, it was concluded to fit out a more formidable expedition in hopes of exterminating this troublesome nest of refugees.

The expedition failed as to its main object, from an ignorance of the real strength of the post, and of the localities, but it resulted in alarming the enemy so much that they soon after abandoned the post.

This affair on account of its failure, is not described in any history of the Revolution, and is barely alluded to in a letter of Washington. This must be my apology for giving a sketch of it from memory as it was detailed to me by an eye-witness, Wm. Ludlam, of Hog Island, who lately died at a very advanced age.

Mr. Ludlam was not a Whig, but from his quiet disposition, continued a Loyalist. His goodness of heart, however, would not allow him to harm any human being, friend or foe. He was just grown at the time of the American defeat at Brooklyn, and out of mere curiosity, walked down to the battle ground, saw the dead, and the ground covered with the scorched paper of which the cartridges had been made.

He was a tailor by trade, and living, as he did, on Hog Island, in an exposed situation, his house, or rather Squire Smith's, with whom he lived, was now and then robbed by Connecticut whale boat men. Once, in the fall of the year, Mr. Ludlam had on hand a large quantity of cloth and made up clothing, the property of the neighboring farmers, which had accumulated on his hands, and which he had not yet had time to return to their respective owners; when suddenly, one night, the door was broke in, the house plundered, and all the garments and cloth carried off! Thus was a whole neighborhood in a measure deprived of their winter clothing and a sorry tale was there for Mr. Ludlam to tell his disappointed customers!

But I am digressing from my story. One fine summer day, in 1845, I crossed in a boat from the pleasant village of Oyster Bay to the residence of the venerable man. He was somewhat dull and careless, at the first few questions I put to him; but when I spoke of olden times and the Revolution, the tears came in his mild and somewhat bedimmed eye, his voice faltered; I had struck a tender chord, had reminded him of the days of his youth—of troublous times. In a few moments he recovered himself, and as the recollection of times long past came to his mind, his conversation took a cheerful and spirited tone. He related anecdotes and adventures of all kinds.

"Come," said he, taking his cane and his broad brimmed hat, "let us go on to the hill and I will describe to you the attack by land and water which the French and Americans made on Lloyd's Neck. I saw it with my own eyes as I was binding wheat sheaves in my harvest field just 64 years ago."

For a clearer understanding of the matter, I made a rude sketch of Hog Island, and of Lloyd's Neck, which lies east of it. When we reached the field at (a), the old gentleman gave me a description of Lloyd's Neck as it was in the Revolution. Pointing with his cane towards (b), "There," said he. "was the Fort built to protect the wood cutters, and used also as a depot for hay and straw which was collected from the adjacent country and shipped to New York. The French fleet landed a party of 250 men at (c), who were to attack the Fort in the rear, but they got bewildered, and when at last they reached the Fort, they found it better defended than their spies had led them to expect. In truth the guns had been mounted only the day before! So unexpectedly did the refugees discharge their grape shot, that the French (who had neglected to bring any artillery) at once retreated, leaving behind some surgeon's instruments, lint, bandages, port-fire, &c., and the grass besmeared with blood.

At the same time with the attack on the rear of the Fort, and to draw off the attention of the British refugees, a French sloop of war hove to at (f), but could bring only one gun to bear on the Fort. She also attempted to cut out a British 10 gun brig that lay at (e) under cover of the guns of the Fort.

The main body of the French fleet, however, after landing the men at (c) sailed into the mouth of Huntington Harbor and attacked some British vessels that had run into a small creek for shelter at (h), a portion of whose crews had already landed and mounted a few guns in battery at (g), by which they hoped to keep off the French shipping. In this they succeeded, for as soon as the French Admiral was apprised of the failure of the attack on the landside of the Fort, he at once abandoned the attempt, sailed to a preconcerted spot, took on board his defeated marines and returned to Newport, saying very little about his repulse. Flaming paragraps were, of course, put forth in Rivington's Royal Gazette, as a terror to the rebels and an encouragement to the King's loyal subjects."

Baron De Reidesel writes to Gen. Delancey, to thank Capt. Young's officers and troops, and Capt. Van Wyck's company of foot, and such of the Queens County militia as turned out for their alertness and willingness to assist Col. Upham. But it grieves him to reproach the Huntington militia for their unwilling conduct and absolute neglect of supporting Col. Upham, commandant of the Fort that was attacked.

First Ref. Prot. Dutch Church at Jamaica, L. I.

HISTORICAL SKETCH
OF THE
FIRST REF. PROT. DUTCH CHURCH,
OF
JAMAICA.

As the Corner Stone of the First Reformed Protestant Dutch Church of Jamaica will this day be laid, we have thought it not inappropriate to insert in our impression of to-day the following brief sketch of the History of this ancient Church and of its ministers—more especially as this paper will be placed with other documents in the Corner Stone.

In 1701-2 Domine Lupardus, Minister of the Reformed Dutch Churches of Kings County died and there was no Dutch minister resident on the Island for three or four years. There had also been a steady emigration of the Dutch from Kings County into the western part of Jamaica and perhaps in other parts of Queens County. Still the particular circumstances under which the Church at Jamaica was organized are now unknown. We do know, however, from the Record of baptisms that a church existed here as early as June 19th, 1702. The officiating minister probably came for the first year or two from New York City at times convenient to himself.

For fourteen years the congregation had no place of worship of their own, but as a stone church had been already built at the expense of the Town, they doubtless used that in common with the Episcopalians and Presbyterians at times mutually agreed upon.

On the 15th of April, 1715, subscription papers were circulated throughout Queens County for building a Reformed Dutch Church in Jamaica, that village being then the county town. Indeed so early as Dec. 29th, 1709, the Church at Jamaica had agreed with the Churches of Kings County for the services of Domines Freeman and Antonides at £40 per annum for which they were to have preaching every third Sunday—twice a day during summer.

On the 15th day of June, 1716, the Church had been completed and seats were allotted to subscribers.

In 1727, the congregation in Queens County wished to be set off from Kings County and have a pastor to themselves, giving as reasons that the congregation was widely dispersed, that more Churches were needed in Queens County to accommodate some who had to travel over 20 miles on the Sabbath, that they were surrounded by Quakers and Anabaptists, that their young people by reason of infrequent worship were going off to other

Churches, intermarrying with the English—all which might be obviated by having more frequent worship and a resident minister.

The immediate result of this petition we do not know, but we find that on the 23d of July, there were four Dutch Churches in Queens County and they agreed to give Domine Van Basten £75 per annum for his services.

On the 19th of April, 1741, the Churches of Queens County had waited nine years for a minister from Holland, but none came. They thereupon made a call on Domine John Henry Goetschius who was installed at Jamaica by Domine Freeman. On the 4th of September of the same year ten acres of land in Jamaica were bought for a Parsonage at a cost of £185.

Domine Goetschius not having been ordained in Holland but by Domine Dorsius of the German Reformed Church, the congregation began to feel doubts of the validity of his official acts, a schism followed, Goetschius resigned and many of the children were baptized over again.

On the 19th of Sept., 1752, the congregations of Queens County united in a call on Thos. Romeyn, a student of Theology, on condition that he should go to Holland for ordination, which he accordingly did and was installed at Jamaica by Domine Verbryck on the 10th day of November, 1754.

Domine Romeyn's first sermon was from Psalms, 119:9. On the 10th of June, 1760, he celebrated the Communion for the 10th time in Jamaica, and on the 30th of November following he preached his farewell discourse from Ephes. 6:24.

There does not appear to have been an immediate successor to Romeyn, as we find on the 18th of April, 1763, that the Rev. Abm. Keteltas received £16.5s. as his half year's salary.

On the 16th of February, 1766, Domine Van de Boelen was installed as Pastor by Domine Van Sinderen—the text was from Heb. 13:7. Domine Boelen's first sermon was from Psalm 31:12. He continued as Pastor of the four Churches till about 1772, though he occasionally preached and baptized till 1780, when being a Loyalist, it is supposed he left the country.

On the 11th of June, 1775, Domine Froeligh was ordained Pastor over the Churches of Queens County by Domine De Ronde at Jamaica. Being a Whig, after 15 months of unsuccessful labor here he fled from the Island to escape the vengeance of the British.

During the Revolution the Church was occupied by the enemy as a store-house, and the Dutch ministers from Kings County occasionally visited the congregations in Queens County and baptized their children. In Jamaica the use of the Episcopal Church was allowed them.

After the war, the Church was repaired and in the early part of 1785 Domine Van Nest was installed. He left in 1797.

On the 13th of July, 1791, Domine Kuypers was ordained by Rev. John H. Livingston at Success, as Co-pastor with Domine Van Nest of the Collegiate Churches of Queens County. The text was appropriate to the season of the year—"The harvest truly is plenteous, but the labourers are few." Domine Kuypers preached his farewell sermon in the same Church, April 10th, 1825, having retired from the charge of the other three Churches at different times previously.

On the 20th of April, 1802, the connexion of the four Dutch Churches of Queens County was terminated; and on the 24th of October following the Rev. Jacob Schoonmaker was ordained by Domine Jackson at Newtown as joint-pastor with Domine Kuypers of the Churches of Newtown and Jamaica. In 1830 Rev. Dr. Schoonmaker resigned the charge of the Church at Jamaica, having relinquished that of Newtown the year before.

The Rev. G. J. Garretson was on the 6th of January, 1835, installed by the Rev. Dr. Strong at Newtown as joint-pastor with Domine Schoonmaker and so continued till June, 1849, when he left the Island.

On the 7th of Jan., 1851, the Rev. J. B. Alliger was installed as Pastor of the Church at Jamaica, by the Rev'd. Dr. Schoonmaker, late Pastor. The Sermon was delivered by the Rev. Jacob Brodhead, D. D., the charge to the Pastor by Rev. E. S. Porter, and the charge to the people by the Rev. Thos. C. Strong.

The old octagon Church that was built in 1715-16, having been repaired from time to time was at last, from the increase of population, found to be too small and otherwise inconvenient; and on the 4th of July, 1832, the corner stone of a new and much larger Church was laid with appropriate ceremonies; and it was solemnly dedicated to the worship of Almighty God on the 4th of July following. This edifice was placed somewhat in the rear of the old one and was (after having been beautifully repaired and painted at an expense of $3,000) totally consumed by fire communicated to it from a neighboring building on the night of the 19th of Nov., 1857—only a few hours after the workmen had completed the repairs

On the destruction of their place of worship the use of the several churches of the village with expressions of sympathy were kindly tendered to the Congregation. The Presbyterian was selected as causing the least inconvenience under all the circumstances, and here the congregation worshipped till the completion of their Consistory Room on Union Avenue, which was dedicated in June, 1858. This the congregation will use for public worship until the completion of a Fire-proof Brick Church whose corner stone (with Divine Permission) will this day be laid.

QUEENS COUNTY IN OLDEN TIMES.

By H. Onderdnok, Jr.

SCHOOLS.

In those days of Union schools, High schools and Institutes, the school boy loses the chances of those pleasant reminiscences of school boy days that have been the theme of many sentimental story. The poetry, the romance is all gone save in a few sequestered nooks of our Island.

In olden times the school-house was the least pretentious of all buildings. No idea of ornament, or embellishment of any kind seemed to occur to our forefathers in the erection of churches and school-houses and yet around them cling pleasant and happy memories.

The school houses, as I have known them, were innocent of paint inside or out, nor were the walls or ceiling plastered. The old fashioned fire place had indeed been supplanted by a close Dutch stove, which strove almost in vain to overcome the cold which rushed in with the wind at every crevice in the floor and wainscot.

The wood was supplied abundantly and in a loose way, usually each parent in rotation carted a load which was expected to be cut up by the larger boys from day to day as wanted. The fire was made in the morning by the first comer from coals he had borrowed from the nearest house, and in the cold weather the schollars were huddled around the stove till nearly noon, when the room would begin to get comfortable.

The larger girls were required to sweep the school which was done about one a week; and once a quarter (or not so often) there was a grand scrubbing time, the larger boys bringing the water and the girls cleaning the floor with brooms.

Two boys with a water-pail suspended on a stick between them usually troubled some neighbors's well for water once or twice a day.

The marked peculiarity of those days was the respect and deference with which children were accustomed to treat their superiors or elders. The moment a respectable man was seen approaching, on the road, the boys and girls arranged themselves in distinct rows and made their obeisance to the passor by who returned the salutation with an inclination of the head and an approving smile, perhaps, adding some pleasant remark. What wholesome sentiment is inculated by such practises compared with our modern specimens of juvenile manners! Too often the wayfarer hears a rude remark, a snow-ball is thrown at his horses, or the boys "hang on behind" as the phrase is.

One of the by-laws of the Academy at Jamaica (1092) runs thus: "When the tutor or any gentlemen comes in or goes out of the school room, every scholar shall rise up with a respectful bow and they shall treat all men, especially known superior, with the greatest modesy and respect."

Why need I speak of those hard benches without backs, made of the solid half of a split-oak tree, those tables with ponderous legs and covered with chesnut planks over two inches thick, on which the scollars had to tread to reach the shelves overhead where were placed their dinner-baskets, hats and overcoats?

The boys sat separately but usually recited in one class, so far as classes were formed; for in those times classification was an art unknown; and not so much needed as at present, for the circle of knowledge as usually taught at schools was confined to the "3 R's, Reading, Riting and Rithmetic."

But the limited range of the sciences was the reason of their being well taught. The old proverb well said: "Beware of a man of one book." As school books were not various, so there was but little choice and thus one book was a text book for generations.

The elementary book used was the Primer (in Latin *Primarius*, meaning the 'first book'), but as that had a scanty supply of spelling lessons and led the learner too abruptly from spelling to reading: and was besides primarily intended for a book of religious teaching, the great book of the day was Dilworth's spelling book, which kept its ground till after the Revolution when Noah Webster supplanted it. Dilworth was a teacher at Wapping, England, in 1740. He was the author of several school books. His arithmetic held its ground longer than his spelling book and was supplanted by Daboll after a 30 years' struggle.

Our teachers were usually from 'the old country,' too often fond of strong drink and kept blue Monday. Some had their bottle hid in the desk and imbibed at pleasure. Their forte was figures and they usually were better Arithmeticians than the New England teachers who superseded them. Arithmetic was not taught in classes, but each scholar plodded on alone, and when his slate was full of sums, he exhibited it to the *master* as he was then called, for approval. They were then copied into a cyphering book. Originally the teacher alone had the printed arithmetic, which was for that reason called the 'Teacher's Assistant,' as supplying him with examples and their solution ; but after a while each scholar supplied himself with an arithmetic, which relieved the teacher of the labor of setting the scholars' sums on their slates. Each of the more advanced scholars had a quire or so of foolscap paper stitched in a paste-board cover, called a cyphering book. In this the master wrote the examples and when the pupil had performed the operation correctly on his slate, they were copied into the cyphering book and kept as an heir loom in the family, and might be used by younger brothers as a Key.

The reading books were more varied. After the easy lessons of the spelling book had been mastered, there came the Psalter, Testament and Bible. In some schools were the child's Instructor, the Young Gentleman and Lady's Monitor.

Then came the American Preceptor; and latterly Murray's Introduction, English Reader and Sequel. The New England Primer was always to be found in the schools, but it was rather used as a Picture Book. The catechism would be learned out of it, and other moral lessons.

Noah Webster formed a grammatical Institute of the English language in three parts, Speller, Reader, and Grammar. The first only kept its ground.

The spelling class was a feature of those days—all the scholars were arranged in a long row once and sometimes twice a day for ~~rivals~~ [a trials] in their skill in orthoepy. This practice certainly produced good spellers. To be 'head of the class' was the hight of a scholar's ambition.

When the New England teachers came elocution was attempted, and the Columbian Orator used as a text book. Feeble attempts at dressing in character were also essayed. Compositions also were introduced but at a later day.

Writing was well attended to and it was good,—a legible round hand. The labor of making pens from quills (for steel pens were unknown) was not inconsiderable, nor had the writing books been ruled with blue ink as at present. Hence the industrious teacher was at his desk every morning a half-hour or so before the formal opening of school to mend and make pens, rule the writing books with a leaden plummet and set copies.

School usually commenced at 8 o'clock in summer and 9 in winter, and with a noon-spell of an hour, was let out at 4. But as only three branches of education were taught, somehow, there seemed to be a good deal of unemployed time. Then the teacher from very listlessness would doze and nod, the scholars for want of better employment read whatever was readable in the school books—perhaps for the twentieth time. By oft ~~attempted~~ [repeated] perusal the very sums in the Arithmetic were learnt by heart—especially the curious examples at the end of the book.

In some schools an intermission was allowed, but more generally each scholar asked for permission to go out, at the same time, turning a tablet or 'block' that hung by the door on the opposite side of which were inscribed 'IN'— 'OUT.'

Grammar was not taught in those times. 'Tis true that at the end of Dilworth's and Webster's spelling books, there were ~~being~~ treatises on English grammar but written on the basis of Latin Grammar, with few or no examples for practise. It may truly be said that the act of teaching English grammar, but written on the basis of Latin Grammar, with few or no examples for practise. It may truly be said that the art of teaching English grammar was but little understood in those days. For in the statutes of the Academy at Jamaica in 1792, it is ordered that the text-book for English Grammar shall be Webster to be read or repeated by memory.

brief

Navigation was taught in the Common Schools, for many of the young men in those days went to sea, some as sailors, some as supercargoes, some studied medicine and established themselves in the West Indies till they had acquired a fortune when they returned and settled in their native place. Thence navigation was a favorite study. Surveying also was not neglected.

Latterly Geography was taught after a fashion almost without maps. Those penduous octavos of Guthrie and Salmon were text books in some Academies and were superseded by Morse. In common schools Dwight's Geography by Question and Answer was used as a reading book.

Astronomy was seldom, if ever, taught. Hence we need not wonder that many persons almost to our day had no faith in the revolution of the earth around the Sun, or on its own axis.

Some of the books used in Academies before 1800 were: Blair's Rhetorick; Stone's Euclid; Martin's Trigonometry; Warden's Mathematics.

In 1792. The use of Globes, Book-keeping, Oratory, Logic and chronology are named as subjects of study in U. H. Academy. We had almost forgotten to speak of the school girl. She too had her enjoyments, though she usually staid home in winter when the "big boy's" took a quarter's schooling. The girls had their baby houses enclosed with a row of stones as may now be seen along the highways, in country places. They made and returned visits and kept house generally. And if there were some pretty gentle boys, they often "played man and wife", for a brief hour or so.

In some schools the catechism was recited, but this was not a prevailing custom. The catechism was generally heard by the clergyman at the church or at a private house in some convenient neighborhood.

Some of the New England Teachers were of a religious turn of mind and they would cause this to be felt in school, and could take part in a prayer meeting. If to this they could add the gift of singing and form singing schools, their fortune was made. They had the *entree* into respectable farmers' families and a favorable chance of a matrimonial aliance with their daughters.

QUEENS COUNTY IN OLDEN TIMES.

By H. Onderdonk, Jr.

THE CLERGY.

The respect paid the clergyman was great. He was not perhaps so much in contact with the people as at present. The respect for rank was universal. The clergy wore bushy wigs, gown and bands, breeches with knee buckles, and a cocked hat. They often rode on horse back owing to the bad roads but sometimes they used a one horse-chaise. Every house then had a horse-block to which the horse was taught "to side up' to let his rider mount. If a mantua-maker was wanted, a man was sent after her on horse back and returned with the lady seated behind him on a pillion. Some horses would not carry double. Our one horse-wagons began to be introduced a little before 1820, and the saddle fell into disuse gradually. But in the palmy days of horse riding, as soon as a boy aspired to become a young man, a new saddle and a handsome young creature was his first outfit. The young men usually rode in couples, and many a neck has been broken by their racing.

It may be said that the people in those times got rich not so much by making money as by saving it. It was a rule in one family—and that not a poor one to make 365 candles last a year. The children went to bed when the chickens went to roost. So one pair of shoes with mending was calculated to last a little girl the year round.

Of course she went barefoot-in warm weather.

Every family had a leach-tub to make ley which was used to make soft soap. The boiling of soap required much attention.

Dipping candles was an operation that required all the care that a prudent housewife could bestow. The tallow must be melted, the candle rods furnished with wicks, the floor cleaned so that the drippings of the tallow may be kept clear of dust and dirt. Two saw benches 8 feet apart support two transverse rails on which rest 25 or 30 candle rods. The woman begins at one end and successively dips the wicks in the pot of tallow, till the candle acquires the proper degrees of thickness.

Breach of promise suit were rare. The first I notice is in 1807, when Rhoda Seaman recovers six cents damages from Simeon Searing. The next case was in 1822, Demott vs. Smith, with a verdict of $2,000.

When a person met with a calamity, such as the burning of his house or barn, it was necessary to get a Permit from the Governor to solicit assistance. In 1729 Mr. Shaw of East Hampton was burnt out and had such a permit. This printed on a broad-side might be read from the pulpit by the minister who then preached a sermon on charity.

Churches were sometimes situated in the Highway, when they were built at the expense of the town and considered town property. The church in Jamaica and Brooklyn, were put in the middle of the road, carriages passing on either side.* These buildings were used for any public business. The old Dutch church that stood in Fulton street within a stone's throw of the City Hall was occupied by Gen. Washington as his Head Quarters during the memorable battle and retreat of Brooklyn. It was in this building that the war council of General officers was held when it was decided to evacuate Long Island and its dependencies.

They were rarely painted inside or out: Pews were rare, but instead were rush-bottomed chairs for women and benches without backs for men. The services were in summer twice a day, with an hour's interval between, during which the people walked about, conversed, took a lunch, or went to a neighboring tavern and called for cake and beer, or something stronger.

The sexton's office was then unknown and not needed, for the floor was sanded, there were no carpets nor cushions, nor chandeliers, nor heating apparatus. The Deacons unlocked the door and with a long rod opened the high window shutters from the outside. The clerk's business besides singing was on the occasion of a baptism, to write out on paper the name of the child and its parents and hand it to the minister and to provide water in a pewter basin.

---

* It is related of Domine Van Zinderen that while preaching, the congregation had their attention diverted from him by two wagons hastily driven one on each side of the church. The Dominee exclaimed "a race!" Whereupon the excitement of the congregation soon subsided.

QUEENS COUNTY IN OLDEN TIMES.

By H. Onderdonk, Jr.

SPORTS.

But the sports of school-boy days should not be forgotten- such as ball, tag, puss in the corner, playing horse, racing, jumping, hopping, quoits, tetering, skating and sliding on the ice, running down hill and snow-balling, for then we had notable snow-storms. The roads were drifted full, the fences covered with snow-banks curved in graceful and fantastic forms by the wind. The fall of snow was the premonitor of joy and jollity among the younger members of the household. All other business gave way. The wood sled and the pleasure sleigh were got out, and errands of all kinds were contrived to put them in requisition—drawing fuel from the woods, grain to the mill, or goods from the store.

The pleasure sleigh with its jingling bells was kept busy in visiting friends—especially those at a distance. Of course the children must stay home from school to share the ride. To accommodate the belles and beaux the country Taverns got up numerous dancing frolics or (in modern parlance) Balls, where the fiddle and giddy dance and supper kept the over-delighted rustics oblivious of the passing hours so long that they seldom got home till morning. Our modern snow-storms are of no account. Then in the absence of India rubbers we had stout greased cow-hide boots; or if shoes, then knit leggins were drawn on the leg coming up to the knee and protecting the ancles from the snow.

The boy who has an eye to gain rises early, draws on his leggins and waddles through the snow to the woods where he has set his box-trap and spring-pole for the rabbit. Sometimes he finds a squirrel has by mistake been decoyed into the trap by the smell of the apple which was set for a bait, and has gnawed his way out of the wooden box and made good his escape. When, however, he secures a couple of squirrels he strips off the skin whole (as near as he can) and turning the fur inside he has a pair of warm winter gloves.

He also sets quail traps made of thin elder rods, or he attaches half a dozen snares of horse-hair to a cord held tense by two sticks driven in the ground. About these he sprinkles chaff with a few grains of wheat. As he visits these before and after school he seldom fails to find some unlucky bird struggling for a larger liberty. These he has been taught to kill by pressing his thumbnail on the brain.

When he sets a trap for the musk-rat that infest our ponds, he will line it with old iron hoops, so that the prisoner may gnaw the iron bars in vain. Of the skin he will make him a warm winter cap.

The skunk he will leave to the negro who dexterously kills him, eats his flesh and extracts from his fat a valuable domestic ointment called "skunk's grease" and highly esteemed.

One of the oldest sports in Queens County is horse racing. The course was at first, 1669, on Salisbury Plains west of the Court House. It was afterwards styled New Market course. There was a race course around the Beaver Pond, Jamaica; also on Ascot Heath, Flatlands. Beside horse racing, we have what is called the sack race, i. e., the persons who are to run are enclosed in a tall bag or sack which is tied about the neck, so that nothing but the head is visible. As a pendant to this we have the greased pig and the greased pole. A pig is greased and let loose. He becomes the property of the man who can catch and hold him by the greased tail. To clamber a pole that has been well slushed is no ordinary feat. From this we see that after a taste for moderate pleasures is gratified, then an inordinate appetite must be satisfied.

When a tavern keeper wants to replenish his purse, he buys a fine fat pig and distributes a certain number of chances at a certain price. Whoever guesses nearest the weight has the pig. On the day of the guessing, a crowd of the lower sort of people assemble, view the pig, discuss his probable weight, take a drink, get lively, drink again and again. The tavern keeper is in no hurry to kill his pig, as long as the drinking and guessing are going on; but when the crowd are talked out and begin to get impatient, the pig is slaughtered in presence of the crowd, weighed and handed over to the lucky guesser, who, perhaps, not knowing what to do with "the elephant," sells him at a low figure to the tavern keeper. He then treats all around and the crowd gradually fall off and retire homeward. So we have shooting or raffling for turkeys, at the Holidays. A colt or other fine animal is often disposed of by raffling.

Fishing, is not only a sport on L. I., but a means of support to great numbers of poor people who "follow the bay," as it is termed. Many of these are gunners and shoot wild fowl as well as catch crabs. The eels are caught with bait in an eel-pot, or in winter are speared [as they lie in the mud] through a hole cut in the ice. On the south shore *skippers*, a coarse clam, are caught, taken from their shells and barrelled up for bait and sold to the New England cod-fisheries. On the north side of the Island the oyster business has greatly increased, and most of the bottoms of the bays are now occupied by beds where young oysters grow for the New York market. In the deep waters and rocks lobsters are trapped and black-fish are caught with hook and line in abundance. What with the hard clams, the soft clams, muscles and scollops it is hardly possible to calculate the value of the Long Island fisheries. Nor should we forget the horse foot so much used in fattening chickens and pigs. Who has not heard of grouse and snipe shooting?

On the Plains we once had plover grounds, but these paling days of the amateur sportsman are now rapidly passing away. The forests are being cut down and the ruthless herd of boys who fire at anything from a chipping bird to a barn-door fowl has frightened away most of the lawful game.

In Suffolk County we yet have deer. Deer hunts were once a great affair. Men divided into companies and pursued the deer according to a system. One party went in the thicket to drive out the animal, while another stood in the road or clearing to shoot him, as soon as he made his appearance. We often read of accidents happening from carelessness. Men being shot instead of the deer.

The shad fishery should not be forgotten— especially as the Narrows was famous for its shad and the name of Cortelyou is memorable for making immense hauls.

Whales have been struck on Rockaway Beach, on Long Island and have passed by Brooklyn up the Hudson River.

For years long past fish have been caught in nets and used for manure, especially in Suffolk County.

The above cut is a representation of the stone meeting house erected by the town of Jamaica, as a common place of worship for its inhabitants in 1699. It stood in the middle of the main street at the head of Union Hall street, then and long after called "Meeting-house lane." The building was taken down in 1813, when the present Presbyterian Church was erected.*

At the first settlement of the town, there were some Independents, but in the course of time the Presbyterian Church prevailed. Church business was transacted at town meetings. Humphrey Underhill and William Creed are the only ones mentioned (in 1674), as not in accord with their fellow-townsmen in church matters.

At a meeting held Jan. 1st, 1694, in order to the building of a meeting house for the town of Jamaica, John Oakey, Samuel Deane, Samuel Denton, Capt. Carpenter and John Smith were chosen a Committee to divide the town into five squadrons, and to see timber, stones and lime all gotten, as shall be necessary for said work. But it was soon found that there was some unwillingness to be taxed for it by the Dutch population, and those at the west of Jamaica; and especially by William Creed, Robert Read, Esq., John Oakey, Daniel Whitehead, Nicholas Everett, Joseph Smith, Jonas Wood, Hendrick Lott, Elderd Lucas, Frederick Hendrickson and Theodorus Polhemus. The matter was left to arbitrators who decided against the objectors, and they had to pay their rates. But the building of the church was delayed; and Sep. 13, 1698, a new Committee was chosen, consisting of Capt. Carpenter, Capt. Woolsey, Jonas Wood, Benjamin Thurston, Capt. Whitehead, Joseph Smith, John Smith, Edward Burroughs and John Hansen, to carry on the work of building a church and see it truly carried out and ended.

When Lord Cornbury became Governor of New York, he claimed the meeting house as the property of the Church of England, and encouraged the Rev. Mr. John Bartow to strive with Rev. Mr. John Hubbard, the Presbyterian incumbent, for the occupancy of the building. Hence occurred a scene which we will allow Mr. Bartow to describe in his own graphic style:

"I once met with great disturbance at Jamaica. Mr. Hubbard, their Presbyterian minister, having been for some time in Boston on a visit, returned to Jamaica, the same Saturday night as I came to it, and sent to me at my lodging (I being then in company with our Chief Justice, Mr. Mompesson, and Mr. Carter, Her Majesty's Comptroller), to know if I intended to preach on the morrow. I sent him answer I did intend it. The next morning (July 28, 1703), the bell rang as usual, but before the last time ringing Mr. Hubbard was got into the church and had begun his service, of which notice was given me, whereupon I went into the church and walked straightway to the pulpit expecting Mr. Hubbard would desist, since he knew I had orders from the Governor to officiate there; but he persisted, and I forbore to make any interruption. In the afternoon I prevented him by beginning the service of the Church of England before he came. He was so surprised when he got to the church door and saw me performing divine service, that he suddenly started back and went aside to an orchard hard by, and sent in some persons to give the word that he would preach under a tree. Then I perceived a whispering through the church, and an uneasiness of many people, some going out, some seemed amazed, and not yet determined to go or stay. In the meantime some that had gone out returned again for their seats; and then we had a shameful disturbance, hauling and tugging of seats, shoving one another off, carrying benches out, and returning for more, so that I was fain to leave off till the disturbance was over, and a separation made; by which time I had lost about half the congregation, the rest remaining devout and attentive the whole time of service. After which we locked the church door and committed the key into the hands of the Sheriff. We were no sooner got into an adjoining house but some persons came to demand the key of their meeting house; which, being refused, they went and broke the glass windows, and put a boy in to open the door, and so they put in their seats, and took away the pulpit cushion, saying they would keep that for their own minister. The scolding and wrangling that ensued are by me ineffable."

The next time I saw my Lord Cornbury, he thanked me for what I had done, and said he would do the Church and me justice. Accordingly he summoned Mr. Hubbard and the heads of the faction before him, and forbade him ever more to preach in the church, for as it was built by a public tax it did appertain to the established church. He also threatened them all with the penalty of the statute for disturbing divine service, but upon their submission and promise of future quietness and peace, he pardoned the offence."

The Presbyterians made other violent attempts to regain possession of the church but failed, and were fined and punished. They worshipped for nearly 25 years in a building erected at the east end of the village, and also in the County Hall. At last they commenced a suit at law, and were successful. This was one of the most important law suits that ever was prosecuted on L. I., and aroused all the bad feelings of the litigants.

In the absence of a full report, we give the minutes of the trial as we find them noted in the private Record book of the Judge before whom the case was tried. They are dry and technical, but they are all we have to give:

"Supreme Court held at Jamaica, Dec. 23, 1728, Lewis Morris Esq. Chief Justice. Stephen Theobalds on the demise of Carpenter and others vs. Thomas Poyer, Rector of the Parish of Jamaica.

EVIDENCE FOR PLAINTIFF.

Nehemiah Smith sworn.
Col. Dongan's Pat. to the inhabitants of Jamaica, read
Zechariah Mills sworn.
Town vote of Jamaica in 1716, to vest the ground on which the church stands, in certain persons, read.
John Foster and Samuel Smith sworn

EVIDENCE FOR DEFENDANTS.

Copy of town vote read.
Copy of warrant for town meeting read
Benjamin Wiggins sworn.
Defendant being called on confesses lease entry and ouster.
A vote in 1699 empowering persons to carry on the building of a meeting house or church.
An Act of Assembly for the erecting a public edifice in 1699, read.
Jonathan Whitehead sworn.
A receipt from the Trustees to Jonathan Whitehead as collector, for money gathered by him in 1702.
Samuel Smith sworn.
An Act for settling a ministry in several towns in the Province, read
A copy of a record of a trial between Thomas Poyer and George McNish, in the Supreme Court, was produced as evidence, and allowed.
A patent from Gov. Nicolls to the inhabitants of Jamaica, read.
A release from Wm. Hallett, the surviving patentee, to Thos. Poyer, for the church or building in dispute, read.
Charles Doughty took his affirmation.

EVIDENCE FOR PLAINTIFF RESUMED.

William Carpenter and Thomas Smith sworn.
Thomas Gale took his affirmation.
Derick Brinckerhoff, John Pettit and Andrew Clark sworn.
A motion of Mr. Berkley, in an inferior Court held at Jamaica, read.
Daniel Whitehead sworn.
Three orders of the town in 1695, read.
Two orders of the town in 1697, read.
Nicholas Berrian sworn.
The jury find for plaintiff 6 pence damages and 7 pence costs.
The process returned, November Term, 1728.

Mr. Poyer's counsel complained of the partiality of the Judge, for he designed to put the matter on some points of law which were in his favor, and in the time of trial offered to demur in law, but was diverted therefrom by the Judge who told him that he would recommend it to the jury to find a special verdict, and if they did not he would then allow a new trial. This he afterwards refused to do, saying a bad promise was better broke than kept.

Note.—For the above drawing we are indebted to the antiquarian taste of Judge David Lamberson. He had carefully drawn it with a lead pencil. He also preserved the vane (a copper rooster), with the figures 1699 inscribed on it.

THE OLD STONE PRESBYTERIAN CHURCH IN JAMAICA.

[CONTINUED FROM STANDARD OF MAY 18.]

[Republished by Request.]

After the Presbyterians recovered their church by process of law (1738), they had undisturbed possession till the Revolution, when it was used for a very short time by the British as a place of detention for Whig prisoners.

Soon after the British army came into Jamaica (1776), a parcel of frolicksome young Loyalists perched themselves in the belfry and commenced sawing off the steeple. Word was brought to the pastor, Mr. Burnet. Whitehead Hicks, Mayor of New York, happened to be staying at the parsonage which stood in the rear of Mr. Lewis' hardware store, in Beaver street, and he soon put a stop to the intended outrage.

Mr. Burnet had married Miss Ann Combs, of Jamaica, an Episcopalian, and was the only Presbyterian minister hereabouts that favored the British cause. He was, therefore, allowed to continue public services in the church during the war. Though he saved the church from destruction, yet after the peace the exasperated Whigs made it uncomfortable for him and he had to leave.

The Highlanders attended his services, and sat in the gallery. Some had their wives with them, and several of their children were baptized. Once when the sexton had forgotten to provide water for baptism, the thoughtful mother pulled a bottle from her pocket and poured the water in the basin.

After the war, and while there was no County Court house, the Judges held their Courts in the old church. Two robbers were here sentenced to death and hanged at Beaver Pond.

The edifice was of stone 40 feet square, and had three doors, and aisles to correspond. The pulpit, surmounted by its sounding-board, stood on the north side facing the gallory. For a time Mr. Bernardus Hendrickson, aged and thick of hearing, sat in the pulpit beside the minister, and wore a woolen cap. The minister had gown and bands. There was no stove. The women (some at least) arrayed in scarlet cloaks, sat on chairs along the wide aisle, and had foot-stoves. The floor was sanded. There was little work for the sexton, Jos. Tuttle, to keep the house in order. So he was content (1791) to take up with a yearly salary of £1 for taking care of the church, and £1 for ringing the bell. The minister's salary was $300, and parsonage with some accidental advantages as marriage fees, spinning parties and special gifts when he had had sickness in his family, or other misfortunes.

There were two services on the Lord's day with an hour's intermission, when the people eat what they had brought from home, or went into Capt. Joseph Roe's bakery (where widow Waters now lives), and regaled themselves on ginger bread and spruce beer. Those that wished something stronger could get it at Wm. Betts' inn, since B. Creed's inn, over the way.

Thomas Bailey, Jos. Tuttle and Chas. S. Lord successively led the singing. Mr. Lord stood in the gallery, the others in front of the pulpit.

In course of time the edifice though often cleaned, repaired, shingled and painted was not thought sufficiently convenient. The old glebe was sold and used as a Female Academy. Richard Creed's house and land was bought (the present parsonage), and May 24, 1813, the workmen began to take down the old stone church against whose walls the Academy boys had played ball for years.

After the rubbish had been removed the ground under the church (especially beneath the communion table in front of the pulpit) was carefully dug over, and the remains of those who had been buried there gathered up and placed in a box and conveyed in procession headed by the sexton, Jeffery Smith, to the village burying place and again committed to the earth. So says the late Chas. B. Shaw, who was present. Among these relics must have been Rev. Patrick Gordon, Rev. Wm. Urquhart, and two wives of Rev. Thomas Poyer.

The new church was dedicated Jan. 18, 1814. The preacher was Rev. Dr. Milledoler, of N. Y. Rufus King was captivated with the discourse and asked Rev. Mr. Sayres, as they were coming out of church, the name of the eloquent divine. "Strange," says he, "that I never heard of him before."

The annexed drawing does not show the building in its original beauty. It had a graceful tapering spire which rose 102 feet from the ground, and could be seen from far. In the course of time some persons thought it had been strained by the September gale of 1821, and that it was racking the frame work of the building, and in spite of the protests of a few objectors, 27 feet of this symmetrical spire was sawn off and ignominiously pulled down by ropes. It fell with a crash and was broken in a thousand pieces, which were gathered in piles and sold for fuel to the highest bidder. Thus was this well proportioned edifice that was peerless among the churches on Long Island shorne of its principal ornament.

For the wood cuts that have illustrated this sketch, we are indebted to the obliging courtesy of Mr. L. M. Jaggar.

*Note —The Presbyterian Church has been fertile in such or similar organizations, as the Cent Society, Society for conversion of the Jews, Bible Society, Union Benevolent, Foreign and Domestic Missions, and many others now passed away and forgotten.

The people had gotten slack and careless, under the failing strength of the good Mr. Fairoute, and few could pray in public. Mr. Weed, fresh from Princeton Seminary, was called in 1815. He quickly infused a new energy in the religious life of his people. He started weekday lectures, prayer meetings, formed a Bible class and (though for a long time before there had been yearly contributions to the Education Society) he prompted the ladies to organize other societies for religious purposes.* The ladies made a beautiful heavy cloth cloak which they presented to him in form. After recovering from his surprise he thanked them for their care of his bodily comfort, and then with an arch smile, he added (as if the cloak were a *douceur*), "ladies, how can I hereafter, in preaching, call you sinners."

Mr. Weed was of acknowledged ability, a preacher of the old school of sterner stuff than ministers now are.

There was no mistaking his notions of a future state especially of the wicked. Smith Hicks who, from a tailor, had become an irreverent publican, used to say he "never knew a preacher who could take up a sinner in both hands, hold him out at arms' length, and so shake him over hell fire as Mr. Weed could."

Hitherto there had been no stove in the church. One Lord's day Mr. Weed broached the subject, and said *he* could stand the cold and keep warm by preaching, but he feared his people would be too uncomfortable to sit and listen patiently to his discourses. So the stoves amid opposition were set up.

Mr. Weed found the hour's intermission too short to rest himself in, and the services were held later in the afternoon. The church had then no lamps for night service, nor sheds for the horses. He let the people know he sought not "theirs but them," and when some one hinted he should be content with less salary, he quietly left.

Mr. Weed discouraged the practice, then prevalent in the best families, of giving wine at funerals. In this he was seconded by Rev. Mr. Sayres. Time out of mind in humbler families rum was handed from one to another as they stood out of doors about the house, each man drinking directly out of the mouth of the up-turned flask; wine was passed around to the women within the house. Capt. Codwise, who lived at Beaver Pond, had a cask of the choicest wine stored away in his cellar for years reserved for his funeral. The last most distinguished occasion in Jamaica was at the funeral of Rufus King, our Minister to England, who died April 29, 1827, at the age of 73. It was a warm day, and the waiters were kept going about, in doors and out, with silver salvers before them loaded with decanters, glasses and segars.

Mr. Weed and Mr. Sayres were (1818) chosen Inspectors of Common Schools for Jamaica. They did their duty so strictly and exposed so many shortcomings in the teachers that they were not re-elected.

Antiquities of Grace Church, No. 4.

THOMAS POYER, Rector of the Parish of Jamaica, 1710 to 1732,

was born in Wales, (a grandson of Col. Poyer who fell in defence of Pembroke Castle in Cromwell's time,) and a student of Brazen Nose College, Oxford. On Sunday, June 9, 1706, he was ordained deacon by Wm. Lloyd, bishop of Worcester, in the parish church of Hartlebury, to serve in the church at Burton in Pembrokshire. On Sunday, Sept. 21, 1707, he was ordained priest by Geo. Bull, bishop of St. Davids, in the chapel of the Virgin Mary in Brecknock. Feb. 21, 1709 he was chaplain of the Antelope at Port Mahon where he had occasion to borrow £7; and Sep. 27, he entered the service of the Society for propagating the Gospel in Foreign parts. Dec. 16, he was appointed to perform at £50 per year all the offices of his sacred function at Jamaica on L. I.; and on Dec. 23d, Henry bishop of London signed his license and a certificate of his subscription of conformity; and on the 30th he embarked; but the fleet was detained till Ap. 10th. He was tossed about from one expensive harbor to another and his wife was twice visited with fits of sickness on board, and he was obliged twice to bring her ashore for the help of a doctor (not a little trouble and charge) and was forced to pay £20 for passage, and twice laying in of sea-stores. He had an uneasy passage of nearly 13 weeks —great tempests, so that he expected to be swallowed up by the merciless waves—and on July 7th the ship and part of her lading was cast away and lost on the shores of L. I. 100 miles from his parish. On the week following he set out for Jamaica where to his surprise he found that his predecessor's widow had not dealt kindly by him; for on the day that he was expected in town she delivered up the parsonage-house to the Dissenters. After his induction into the church (July 18, 1710) by Rev. John Sharpe chaplain of Her Majesty's forces in N. Y., Mr. Poyer made complaint to a Justice of the peace who repaired to the parsonage but could get no admittance, whereupon he made a second record of forceable detainer on his own view, and issued a warrant to the sheriff to apprehend the offenders, but he being a strong Independent refused, so the offenders escaped punishment and Mr. Poyer was kept out of the glebe. It afterwards appeared that widow Urquhart connived at their entry as she was readmitted as a tenant to them, with Benj. Woolsey an Independent student and approbationer who had married Mary Burroughs the widow's daughter by a former husband. Mr. Poyer again in 1712 served the occupant, Rev. Geo. McNish, with a lease of ejectment for continuing his claim. His people on account of his tedious voyage and shipwreck made him a private contribution of about £18.

Mr. Poyer at his first setting out fell into the hands of Mr. Samuel Clowes a practising lawyer and storekeeper, being led by his great zeal for the church, and lodged in his house; but soon changed his lodgings as few of his communion desired to visit him there. He seems afterwards to have lived in a hired house many years; for in 1722 he leased for 2 years more at £15 a year the place of widow Elizabeth Waters which he then occupied on the west side of the road to Flushing.

Soon after induction Mr. Poyer set about his work. He distributed the books given him for that purpose by the Ven. Society, took down the names of the recipients so as to look after them and gave private advice as he went from house to house and taught the fundamentals of religion.

In Jamaica the Dutch had a quarrel among themselves about their minister. Other Dissenters had not got over their vexation at being forced to a tax toward building the public or town meeting-house in 1699, and showed their dissatisfaction with their brethren by appearing in the interest of the Church of England, thinking no way so effectual as that, to spite their former adversaries. These with a few professed churchmen formed the nucleus of the church in Jamaica. In 1702 over 50 (disaffected) persons signed a petition to Lord Cornbury to have constant Lectures among them for the advancement of true religion and the best of churches (the Church of England) and the reconciling of their unhappy differences.

Mr. Poyer preached in turn at Jamaica once a fortnight, Flushing and Newtown once a month. In 1714 he reports that the church increases beyond expectation, he has gained over some Independents, the communicants have risen from 30 up to 60, and among the Quakers in Flushing (where Urquhart did not think it worth while to go) he seldom has so few as 50 and often more than 100 hearers.

The minister's rate from the parish was £60 this country money per year, equal to £39 sterling. The Vestry being chosen by the freeholders was a civil rather than religious body and were usually Dissenters, who refused to pay Mr. Poyer except as he sued and recovered from time to time. In 1710, Oct. 27, by Mr. Clowes he sued for a quarter's salary, but was cast with costs of suit. In 1714 he had not yet received a penny. The Vestry met to lay the Poor and Minister's tax and would not admit him among them. As Judge and Jury (he feared) were not favorable to the church, he thought suits not advisable, and wrote for directions to the Ven. Society who (1715) ordered him to proceed in a suit at law for his salary, at their charge, and made him a present of £30 so that he might bear up under his difficulties. In 1716 he sued and recovered £16.11 from the church wardens. In 1719 the Justices fined and turned out John Everett and Thos. Hazard the church wardens, for refusing to pay the money in their hands to Mr. Poyer, and put Sam. Clowes and Thos. Willett in their room. In 1716 he got a verdict in the Supreme Court before Judge Lewis Morris against the Rev. Mr. McNish for part of his salary: and he expected no further trouble about the rest of it, but the church wardens being obstinate Independents put him to as much or more trouble in suing (1721) for the £45 in their hands.

PARISH.

In 1717 Mr. Poyer complains of his large parish. It is 15 miles long and 6 ½ broad and has 409 families in it; but not above 80 come to church; he has 400 hearers and 60 communicants, has worn out 2 gowns and cassocks, and the third very bare; and his family wants are such that he don't know how he shall get another. (The Ven. Society sent him a gown and cassock and £10 in goods or money as he chose.) He says a missionary should be hospitable which removes the prejudice of some, and brings others over to the church. He has strained himself in traveling thro' the parish even beyond his strength and to the prejudice of his health for almost 7 years, and not received a farthing salary allowed by law. At divers times he has had gifts not amounting to £20. It is a dear place to live and things are costly. He lives below the character of a Missionary and yet runs in debt.

SERVICES.

"I give frequent lectures on week-days, many live 12 miles distant, and I must keep two horses which is expensive and troublesome, and this wears out more clothes in one year than would last 3 or 4, if I did not have to ride. In Newtown and Flushing there is no convenience of private houses, so I have to use public inns at very great charge, for I usually bring some of my family with me. I have service (1724) every Lord's day and on the days set apart by the church. I have communion 4 or 5 times a year or oftener, as I have health, and seldom have over 40 communicants at a time. I catechise all such as are sent to me twice a week in the church, and once a fortnight the year round at my house."

ILL TREATMENT.

At first he had to put up with abuses and affronts from his opponents. He says (1718) "they try to tire me out with their ill usage. I am denied victuals for my money. The miller wouldn't grind my corn, but sent it home and said I might eat it whole as hogs do. They say if the constables offer to collect my salary they will scald 'em, stone 'em and go to club-law with them, &c.

This threat was soon carried out; for on Dec. 5, 1718 as the constable Ri. Combs, went to Daniel Bull's and demanded the rate, he took up an axe and swinging it over Combs' head, said he would split his head if he touched anything there. The constable commanded Jacamiah Denton in the *King's* name to assist him, but he laughed, said he was no constable and wouldn't obey him. He then went up and down the town and mustered 16 or 17 people with Justices Clement & Whitehead and on coming before Bull's door saw him with Wm. Carman, Samuel and Henry Ludlum, Robert and Hezekiah Denton and Ephriam Smith standing there with great clubs in their hands and stript to their waistcoats. On the constable saying he had come to distrain they lifted up their clubs and bid him come if he durst, and gave him scurrilous language. On seeing that Bull had between 20 and 30 persons in his company the constable walked off, and made no distress. The Rev. Geo. McNish bid the people not mind the constable and even invited them into his house to drink cider. These rioters were subsequently let off with a small fine on promise of future peaceable behaviour. Samuel Clowes acted in the absence of the King's attorney.

RYE.

Mr. Poyer had often served the church at Rye, in 1719–20, and it is no wonder he desired an appointment there, tho' Jamaica, he says, "is a much pleasanter place where I have abundantly better conversation than can be had at Rye." He also had invitations to the West Indies and between £400 and £500 per annum offered him.

SUIT FOR PARSONAGE.

In 1724 Oct. 29 Mr. Poyer brought suit against the tenants of the parsonage lands, homestead and outlands, in which he was cast.

We give the minutes of the trial from the Judge's book.

At a court by Nisi Prius held at Jamaica, present Lewis Morris, Esq., Chief Justice.

John Chambers vs Joseph Hegeman, Jr.
The same vs Robert Denton.

Defendants confess lease, entry and ouster.

Evidence for plaintiff.

Thomas Welling, John Dean, Nehemiah Smith sworn.

A vote of town meeting, in 1676 for parsonage lands.

Richard Combs.

Warrant from Lord Cornbury to Ralph Cardale to survey church lands.

Act of Assembly to settle a ministry in Queens Co. (1693)

An act of Assembly to explain the former Act, (1705.)

John Chambers sworn, and Thos. Whitehead.

An exemplification of the special verdict, road,

Evidence for defence.

Agreement of the town of Jamaica with Rev. John Prudden, read.

Votes of the town for Rev. John Hubbard and Geo. McNish to be ministers, read.

Joseph Smith and Elizabeth Stillwell sworn.

Mr. Prudden's exchange of land with the town, (Sept. 29, 1693) read.

Jury find for defendant. Murry for plaintiff and Jamieson for defendant.

The postea returned up Nov. term, 1724.

Antiquities of Grace Church, No. 5.

THOMAS POYER, Rector of the Parish of Jamaica, 1710 to 1732.

TESTIMONIAL.

In 1716, Feb. 6th, while Mr. Poyer was in the midst of his troubles a letter was sent in his behalf to the Ven. Society testifying to his services and hardships, and commending him to their favorable notice, signed by his parishioners: Joel Burroughs, John Clement, Jer. Garronge, Jos. & Wm. Hallett, Jas. Hazard, Thos. Howell, tailor, Jona. Morrell, Fr. Nicolls innkeeper, Ri. Power, Thos. Rattoon, Thos. Smith, Wm. Stroud, Thos. Wiggins, Jona. Whitehead, Thos. Willett, sr., and jr., Thos. Woolsey.

COMMUNICANTS, 1725-7.

Justice Betts and wife.; brother and sister to Madam Clarke; Andrew Mr. Clowes.
Clarke and wife. Sam. Smith and wife.
Justice Clement & wife. Mrs. Arthur Smith.
Mr. Clowes and wife, Mrs. Katrina Stilwell, son Samuel; Gerard- innkeeper.
us; Mrs. Clowes and Mrs. Stroud.
son John. Mr. Taylor.
Mr. Comes. Mrs. Wm. Thorne.
Daniel Denton and wife. Foster Waters and wife.
John Hutchins. Mr. Wiggins and daughter Bedford; Mrs. Isa-
Christopher Kernan.
Capt. Luff. bel Wiggins; Thos.
Judith the negress. Wiggins and wife;
D. Mills. Catharine Wiggins.
Mr. Power. Mrs. Williamson and
Mrs. Poyer. daughter Mary, and
Mr. Reynolds. her two daughters.
Mrs. Sawyer. Col. Thos. Willett; Edward Willett and wife.
Mr. Smith and wife,

At the Communion (1727) the wine cost 3s, the bread 4½ pence. The offering money varied at times from 14s. 2. to 32s. 9. In 1725 the wages of Phillip LeGross, Capt. Luff's servant, the bell-ringer, was 40s. a year. To a poor man traveling to New England 1s. 6 was given, and 6d. to a poor man that was frozen. To Mrs. Stroud in 1722, 5s. was given, and in 1723, 4s. Of the sacrament money on Whitsunday (1722) 6s. 10 in provisions was given to widow Bull.

LIBRARY.

Mr. Poyer speaks of having a Parochial Library. He takes great care of the books and lends them out. Many of his own books the borrowers were slow in returning. He lent John Cross a book 1731, to Mrs. Williamson a pious book, to Sam. Smith at Little Plains "Dr. Littis on prayer." The prayer books furnished by the Ven. Society he gave freely.

SERVANTS.

Mr. Poyer always kept servants, and taught them the Catechism. In 1718, Nicholas Tedry a Palatine was bound to him; a poor widow Angel Spreet (1717) was indentured to him for a term of years, probably to pay the Captain for her passage from England. In 1715 he had his negro slaves Sarah, Phillis and Henry baptized. In 1716 he bought a negro Simon for £41, and in 1718 he had Judith, daughter of this Simon and Sarah baptized. Most churchmen in those days thought it their duty to have their slaves initiated in the christian church.

SCHOOLS.

Mr. Poyer says (1724) there were schools in each town of his Parish, but kept by Presbyterian or Quaker masters. In 1726, at a Town Meeting it was voted by a majority that Mr. Poyer, Mr. Robert Cross the Presbyterian minister, Justices Betts, Messenger and Smith should see what the people are willing to subscribe toward the encouragement of a "Free School" in Jamaica. Probably nothing came of this. Mr. Poyer sent his oldest son Daniel, July, 1731, to Thomas Temple, and in Oct. he was kept home from Mr. Rock's school on account of small pox.

WIVES.

Mr. Poyer was thrice married. His first wife Frances he brought with him over sea. She was buried Ap. 15, 1719, in the old stone church, and May 10, P. M., he preached her funeral sermon wherein he commemorates her virtues. He says: "She endured with so much christian patience her pains and sickness which rendered the latter part of her life nothing else but a long continued death." In Sep. 1720, he visited Boston whence he brought back, as is said, a 2d wife, a widow Foxcroft. His 3rd wife was Sarah, daughter of Justice Jos. Oldfield, gent. a wealthy farmer of Jamaica. Her sister Mary mar'd. Robert Cross, a Presbyterian minister.

CHILDREN.

Mr. Poyer's eldest son Daniel returned to the old country, as is said, on the death of his father. By his last wife he had 4 children, viz: Joseph Oldfield born 1725, and died 1730*; Thomas, born 1726, was a cordwainer, mar'd. 1758, Margaret Hicks of Rockaway (he was overseer of highways in 1760), and afterwards removed to Fishkill; John, born 1728, mar'd. Mary Rhodes of Jamaica and went to Jersey; Sarah, born 1731, mar'd. 1760, Aaron Van Nostrand sexton of the church, who left a list of his interments in the church yard from 1773 to 1820. To his daughter Caty we are indebted for the pious care of her grandfather's numerous papers, which have enabled us to trace this outline of his services in the parish of Jamaica. Unhappily these papers left in custody of Parson Johnson seem to be irretrievably lost. His portrait is in Brooklyn.

NOTE.—*In those days it was customary to hand around wine and other liquors at funerals. On this occasion Mr. Poyer paid 17s. 6 for five gallons of rum.

FARM.

Mr. Poyer must have inherited land or some other property at the death of his wife's father in 1726. He had lived in a hired house most of his life but latterly he had a farm of 53 acres west of Beaver Pond, (since the Codwise property) of which (in 1730) he sold 16 acres to Benj. Woolsey. It was bounded south and west by Wm. Oldfield's land, north and east by highways. In 1715 he bought a 10 acre lot of Sam. Denton, which he sold in 1719, for £26.

RECORDS.

Mr. Poyer's church records beginning July 22, 1710 and ending Dec. 17, 1731, contain entries of the baptisms, marriages and deaths of his people, all neatly written. From 1719 to 1725 there are unaccountable breaks, and scanty entries at distant intervals. He may have been sick, or serving the church at Rye or absent elsewhere. He certainly went travelling to New England. He left a pile of sermons, his diploma, certificates of ordination, list of communicants, also deeds, letters and business papers.

SERMONS.

Such of Mr. Poyer's sermons as have come down to us seem to be well composed. At the end of each he notes when, where, and on what occasion it was delivered. The more notable ones are as follows:

1709, Nov. 13 and 20—at Plymouth, Eng.
1712, Wednesday, May 21 —Thanksgiving for deliverance from being murdered by

negro slaves in N. Y., commonly called "the Negro plot."

1713, Feb. 5—funeral sermon on death Mrs. Rebecca Woolsey age 93.

1714, Ap. 25—sermon in N. Y. before the Governor and his lady.

1714, June 13—sermon at the residence of the Gov'r and lady.

1715, Ap. 7—Thanksgiving for the Accession of King George to the throne, by order of Gov. Hunter.

1716, June 28,—Thanksgiving for the overthrow of the enemies of church and state in North Britain.

1717, Aug. 4—sermon at Elizabeth Town, N. J.

1719, May 10—his wife's funeral sermon.

1720, Sep.—sermon at Boston. Sermon at Burlington, N. Jersey.

1722, Nov. 27—sermon at Lloyd's Neck.

1725, Jan. 9—read a brief for Helena Semiss of Flushing, who had been burnt out.

1727, Nov. 5—Thanksgiving for victory over the Rebels.

AFFLICTIONS.

Mr. Poyer writes (Nov. 9, 1722) "I was so ill as to have little hopes of recovery, indeed I have been in poor health for several years last past;" and again (Oct. 8, 1724) "my life has been one continued scene of trouble, kept out of my allowance from the country for years, and some of it lost; a great deal of sickness I had myself and in my family, seldom all of us being in health at the same time; I have buried 2 wives and 2 children in less than 5 years, and am now eleven in family, the oldest (Daniel) a little over 16, my house rent £16 per year, and an expense every other Sunday of taking my children with me to Newtown and Flushing." June 7, 1731, he was in custody of the sheriff for a judgment of £42 obtained against him by Henry Cuyler, merchant, of N. Y. In 1724 he was cast in the suit for the parsonage, and it 1728 he was deprived of the church and had to preach in the County Court House. Need we wonder that he writes (June 16, 1731) that the infirmities of age bear very hard on him, he is almost unable to officiate and prays the Ven. Society to be permitted to quit his mission and return to Great Britain

The Ven. Society granted his request to return to his native land and appointed Rev. Thos. Colgan catechist to the negroes in Trinity Church, N. Y., to succeed him; but meantime Mr. Poyer had entered into rest.

DEATH.

Mr. Poyer labored in the parish over 21

years and did not put off his harness till Dec. 17, 1731. He seems to have been taken sick suddenly, perhaps with small-pox as it was then prevalent. Dr. Evan Jones, a quaker, was his family physician.† He made his will Jan. 8, 1732, but was so ill that he could not write out his name in full; and died a few weeks after. His age is not given. He was buried (as is said) on the north side of the village Burying ground. No stone marks his grave or that of his widow. Two of his wives were laid under the old stone church while he yet had possession. He bore the character of a good natured, honest man and beneficent to his neighbors.

NOTE.—† Dr. Jones lived on pleasant terms with Mr. Poyer. A note of his yet remains which he sent Mr. Poyer saying he expects some company to dinner and begs of Mr. Poyer some heads of cauliflower to set off his table.

WILL.

In God's name, Amen. I Thomas Poyer, Clerk, being sick and weak, but of sound mind and memory make this my last will and testament.

1st. I give my soul to God, my body to be christianly buried, in certain hopes of a re-union of my body and soul at the last day, and of eternal live through the sole merits of Christ my Saviour; and

2d. My worldly estate, real and personal, I give to my dear wife Sarah and her heirs, who has hereby power to sell such part as she pleases of my real estate for payment of my debts, and the rest of my estate for the maintenance of herself and my children, and to be distributed amongst them at her discretion; and I appoint her Executrix.

Witness my hand and seal this 8th day of January, Anno Domini, 1731.

   The mark of ———
    T. P. | L. S.
   Thomas Poyer. ———

Signed, sealed, delivered and published by the within named Thomas Poyer as his last will and testament, in presence of us

   SAMUEL CLOWES.
   WM. OLDFIELD.
   EVAN JONES.

Proved at Hempstead, Ap. 22, 1732, before the Hon. Geo. Clarke. Letters granted to Sarah Poyer, Executrix.

NOTICE IN N. Y. GAZETTE, May 1, 1752.

All persons having any demands on the estate of the Rev. Mr. Thos. Poyer, deceased, late Rector of the church at Jamaica, are desired to send their accounts to his widow in order for their being satisfied.

☞ Those persons who have borrowed any books of Mr. Poyer are desired to return them immediately.

VENDUE.

The house where Mr. Poyer lately lived in, at Jamaica, with a lot of land thereto adjoining; his household goods, books and other things will be sold at public vendue to the highest bidders on Monday, the 30th day of May next, 1732.

WIDOW POYER.

Mrs. Poyer sold her homestead with 16 acres of land west side of Beaver Pond to the Rev. Thos. Colgan. After paying her husband's debts and settling up the estate she found herself greatly reduced and even in want of the necessaries of life. She had lived in a plentiful state before marriage. She was yet living in 1743. One of the subscription papers for her relief has the following contributions:

	s.	d.		s.	d.
Rev. Thos. Colgan,		6	John Hutchings,		2
Andrew Clarke,	22		Mr. Clowes,		5
Benj. Wiggins,		6	Mrs. Bridges,		1
Ri. Everett,		1	John Betts,		5
Ri. Greene,		1			

Antiquities of Grace Church, No. 6.

REV. THOMAS COLGAN.

Rector of the Parish, 1733 to 1755; was born in England, 1701, and came over in 1725. On the death of Mr. Poyer, Rev. Alex'r Campbell, Miss. at Brookhaven, desired the succession; but the Rector and Wardens of Trinity Church, N. Y., having recommended Mr. Colgan, who had already begun to preach here since June, 1732, Gov. Cosby issued a mandate for his induction on Wed. Jan 31, 1733. He had a clear, distinct and loud voice that could reach the remotest hearers in the church.

MARRIAGE.

Mr. Colgan by his marriage with Mary, daughter of John Reade and money acquired thereby, took a higher position in the social circle than Mr. Poyer.* His children were Reade; Mary, who mar'd. Christopher Smith owner of the place since Gov'r. King's; Sarah, who mar'd. 1761, Thos. Hammersly; Jane, who mar'd. 1760, Wynant Van Zandt; Judith, Thomas and Fleming; John died in 1758.

NOTE.—* Mr. Poyer desired in 1719 an appointment over the church at Rye, though he says: 'Jamaica is a much pleasanter place, where I have abundantly better conversation than can be had at Rye." He officiated at Rye statedly in 1720-1; and on Feb. 28, rec'd. for his services £12, 10. and the Vestry agreed to continue him.

FARM.

He bought the farm of Widow Poyer and

added other land to it so that it was increased to 66 acres, all in good fence, with barn and orchard of 100 trees capable of producing 100 barrels of cider a year. The house had eight rooms on a floor and two good rooms up stairs, sash windows, having a beautiful view of Beaver Pond, more attractive then than now as it was overgrown with shrubs and bushes and was a resort of birds and wild fowl. His widow offered this for sale in 1759, and in 1765 was residing in another house in the village east of and adjoining the Dutch and nearly opposite the English church. She died in April 1776, aged 67. She and her husband were each honored with obituaries in the N. Y. Mercury.

SCHOOLS.

In 1732 the Ven. Society voted £15 a year to Mr. Willett who was of exemplary life and conversation and taught school with diligence. In 1737 he had 43 scholars, of whom 23 were taught gratis by the bounty of the Society. Thos. Temple was also a teacher here at this , from 1731 to 1746. In 1713 John Moore a graduate of Yale College and candidate for Holy Orders was recommended to the Society by Vesey and Colgan as the most proper person to succeed to the vacant school at Jamaica, £15 a year was granted him. In 1761 "the old school house" was sold for £3.

STATE OF THE CHURCH.

During Mr. Colgan's ministration here we hear of no complaints of non-payment of salary, no riots, no lawsuits or quarrels, as was the case with his predecessor. He writes to the Ven. Society (Feb. 16, 1732,) that his congregation increases very much. Before he came to Jamaica but 20 or 30 came to church, now there are more than 200 every Sunday. They join in the worship with decency and devotion. If he had a church instead of a Court House the congregation would be still larger. And again (June 14, 1731) he says he found the church declining, the Quakers and Independents were busy by many studied arts to destroy the christian religion. The people being destitute of a church assembled 3 or 4 years in the Town House, a very improper place for Divine worship, so that many were discouraged from doing their duty on the Lord's Day. He served them near 2 years in this condition, and then they began to exert themselves towards building a new church and solicited help from abroad and especially from the Gov'r and his family.

GRACE CHURCH DEDICATED.

On Friday, April 5th, 1734, the new erected church at Jamaica was opened by the name of GRACE CHURCH, and Divine service performed therein for the first time. The minister of the Parish, the Rev. Mr. Thos. Colgan, preached a sermon upon the occasion from Genesis 28: 16, 17, "Surely the Lord is in this place, etc." His Excellency Gov'r. Cosby, his lady and whole family were pleased to honor the meeting with their presence, and by their very generous benefaction great encouragement was given to a cheerful contribution for the finishing and completing so good a work—a work dedicated to the service of God. The militia was under arms to attend His Excellency, and so great a concourse of people met, that the church was not near able to contain the number.

"After the sermon was ended His Excellency and family, and several ladies, gentlemen and clergy, were very splendidly entertained at the house of Mr. Samuel Clowes, a tavern, in same town, by the members of the said church."—*Bradford's N. Y. Gazette.*

The Governor's lady gave cloths for the pulpit, reading desk and communion table; also a large Bible, Prayer Book and Surplice.

Mr. Colgan further writes: "We worship in the church, which 'tis thought will be one of the handsomest in North America; but it is not yet complete. We want a bell. Our church is flourishing and many are added to it. We are at peace with the Sectaries around us. I shall be of a loving charitable demeanor to every Persuasion." In 1735, Feb. 18, he says the Independents who formerly thro' prejudice thought it a crime to join with us in worship, now freely and with seeming sanctity and satisfaction come to our church when there is no service in their meeting house. I have baptized several grown people. I want some Prayer Books and books of instruction for the poor and ignorant people; and Dr. King's "Invasion of men in the worship of God." A church was erected in Newtown, April, 1735.

PURCHASERS OF PEWS.

Conditions of the sale of the pews and

lots of Grace Church, this 23d of Feb. 1737, viz:

1. Each pew lot to be struck off to the highest bidder.

2. Every purchaser to build [his pew] in such season that the work be not hindered.

3. Every purchaser to make use of his pew, or the church shall let it out to another.

4. On the purchaser leaving the Parish the pew or lot is to revert to the church.

No.		s.	d.	No.		s.	d.
3	Rich. Betts.	10	10	1	Wm. Steel	12	
7	Rich. Betts, jr	11	6	18	Benj. Taylor	9	
	Timthy Bettues	15		20	Benj. Thorne	14	
13	Andrew Clark	12		23	Isaac Van Hook	11	
10	Sam. Clowes, sr	16	10	6	Anth'y Waters	12	
9	Sam. Clowes, jr	11	6		Wm. Welling	18	
	Sam. Clowes	11	6	1	Dan. Whitehead	20	
14	Rob. ..man			39	Benj. Whitehead	20	
23	Thos. Colgan	21	6	17	Edward Willett	3	
2	Rob. Howell	16		12	John Willett	12	
11	Gabriel ...	12		27	Wm. Wiggins *	12	6
19	Sarah Poyer, gratis.			29	Silas Wiggins *	13	
5	Geo. Reynolds	12		16	Henry Wright	10	
25	Dan. Sawyer	11	6	25	Guy Youngs *	14	
	Sam. Smith	5					

Note.—*Defaulted in payment.

CHURCH BELL.

The Jamaica Lottery will be drawn on Nov. 10th, 1747, in Queens County Hall, in the presence of 3 or more Justices of the peace and such other persons as the adventurers may nominate. The managers, Dr. Jacob Ogden and Sam. Clowes give their trouble *gratis*. There are 1300 tickets at 8s. each, equal to £520. From each prize 12½ per cent. will be deducted for purchasing a bell for Grace Church.

1740, Nov. 22, Mr. Colgan writes that the church members have increased yearly for the past 7 years, the building is generally well filled. The Sects look on the church with a more respectful eye. Whitefield and itinerant enthusiasts have lately been preaching on the Island and broach erroneous opinions on regeneration. He wants the Society to send him, for circulation among the people Waterland's pieces and the Bishop of London's Pastoral letter on lukewarmness and enthusiasm. Mar. 24, 1743, he wants "Trial of Whitefield's spirit," "Englishmen directed in choice of religion," "Stillingfleet on separation." Sep. 29th, he again writes that the church was never so thriving and increases in members and in the esteem of those without its pale; he has baptized 17 persons in 3 families tainted with Anabaptism and Quakerism. In 1744, he says: "Our church is peaceful and growing while other separate assemblies are in confusion" * In 1746 he says: "An entire family of good repute has conformed from Independency to our church." A church has been erected at Flushing mainly by the bounty of Capt. Wentworth. A Quaker gave some money at the opening of the new church and afterwards thought he had not put enough in the plate and gave more to the collector. In 1751, Mr. C. speaks of having "50 steady communicants, has baptized 16 whites and 10 negroes in the last 6 months; and 1753 he baptized 12 white and 8 black infants in the last 6 months; and all the 3 churches of his cure are in an increasing state." This is Mr. Colgan's last letter. He died in Dec. 1755, "a gentleman much esteemed by his acquaintance," and was buried in the chancel.

NOTE.—*This alludes to a dissension in the Dutch Churches caused by a sharp sermon of Domine Goetschius, Aug. 22, 1741, on "the Unknown God."

DISPUTED SUCCESSION.

The Rev. Mr. Chandler writes (Ap. 10, 1756) to the Ven. Society that several of the Missionaries had agreed to take their turns in taking care of the Church at Jamaica town till the disputes raised by the Vestry about a successor to Mr. Colgan should subside and a new minister be appointed to officiate there.

Mr. Barclay acquaints the Ven. Society that the church had suffered a great loss by the death of Mr. Colgan at Jamaica, and that the churches under his care were very apprehensive of great difficulties in obtaining a worthy clergyman of the Church of England to succeed him, because the Dissenters were a majority in the Vestry of the Parish; and it too soon appeared that their apprehensions were not without good reason, for the Dissenters prevailed by their majority in the Vestry to present one Simon Horton a Dissenting Teacher to Sir Charles Hardy the Gov'r. for Induction into the Parish of Jamaica town; but the Gov'r. in obedience to his instructions from His Majesty would not admit him into that cure, because he could not produce a certificate under the Episcopal seal of the Bishop of London of his conformity to the Liturgy of the Church of England; and when no person thus qualified had been presented to the Gov'r. after more than six months His Excellency was pleased to collate the Rev. Mr. Samuel Sea-

bury, jr., Missionary at New Brunswick to
the cure of the church at Jamaica town, and
he hath now for some time been settled
there with the society's approbation. *

NOTE. Mr. Seabury (Oct. 12, 1756,) mar'd.
widow Mary Hicks of N. Y. He was son of the
minister at Hempstead by whose influence perhaps
he became Rector of Jamaica Parish. He
was afterwards bishop.

Antiquities of Grace Church, No. 7.

SAMUEL SEABURY, JR., Rector, Easterday, 1757, to Dec. 1766.

STATE OF THE CHURCH.

Mr. Seabury* writes (1759) that within 6 months he had baptized one white and one negro adult, and 15 white and 3 negro infants, but gained no communicants. Preaching once in 3 weeks only keeps up a languid sense of religion. Open infidelity has not made such progress at Jamaica as at Flushing; but the people are remiss in attending Divine service. In 1760 he still complains of the backwardness of church members in attending and of such a neglect of the Lord's Supper that the communicants scarce exceed 20. He labors publicly and privately to bring them to a sense of their duty.

NOTE.*—Originally written Sedborough.

CHARTER.

The following church members thinking its interests and prosperity would be promoted and its temporalities better managed petitioned (Ap. 8, 1761) for a charter.

Samuel Seabury, Jr., Minister.

Rich. Betts.	Jos. Oldfield, sr. and jr.
Thos. Braine.	Adam Lawrence.
Benj. Carpenter,	Wm. Sherlock.
John & Gilbert Comes.	John & Sam. Smith.
Robert Howell.	John Troup.
Thos. Hinchman.	Thos. Truxton.
John Hutchings.	Isaac Van Hook.
Dr. John Innes.	Benj. Whitehead.
Dr. Jacob Ogden.	

STATE OF THE CHURCH.

Mr. Seabury (1762) informs the Ven. Society that the church gradually increases and a more serious turn of mind begins to show itself. The church has been completely repaired, chiefly at the expense of Mr. John Troupe, a worthy gentleman from N. Y., and it is now one of the neatest and most commodious churches in this part of the world. Mr. Troup also presented a silver collection plate, cost £11 2. 8., a large Prayer Book, cost £3 3., and a table for the communion. The entire Parish consists of about 710 ratable inhabitants. About 120 families profess themselves of the Church of England; more than 500 are Dissenters, including quakers, deists and members of the Dutch church, besides 3 families of French Neutrals from Nova Scotia, and a few negroes and Indians. Within the year he has baptized 27 white and 3 negro children and 3 adults. He has 29 communicants. He lately baptized 2 female children of a Jew, a gentleman of fortune in Jamaica town, whose mother is a professor of the Church of England. The father was present and seemed not a little affected.

SUBSCRIPTIONS

for repairing the church steeple, windows, and fence, May 1, 1761:

	£	s.		£	s.
John Armstrong,	1		Dr. John Innes,	4	
John Betts,	5		Thos. Jones,	2	
Rich. Betts,	2		John Jauncey,	1	10
Thos. Betts,	2		Wm. Murray,	1	4
Wm. Betts,		16	Dr. Jacob Ogden,	2	10
Thos. Braine,	2	10	Jos. Oldfield,	2	
John Burnett,			Tunis Polhemus,		16
Benj. Carpenter,	2		Jos. Robinson,	2	
John Comes,	2		Sam. Smith, jr.	2	
Thos. Cornell, jr.	1	10	John Smith, *Union*	2	
Fleming Colgan,	3		Wm. Sherlock,	2	
Geo. Dunbar,		8	John Troup,	10	
Judge Dan. Horsmanden,		10	Robert Troup,	1	10
			Thos. Truxton,	4	
Thos. Hinchman,	2		Ph. VanCourtland	1	10
Wm. Howard,	1		Isaac Van Hook,		10
Thos. Hammersly,	1	5	Benj. Whitehead,	2	10
Hutchings & Howell		16			

FARM.

"Feb. 1. 1762. To be sold and entered on when the purchaser pleases, a small plantation (since Walter Nichols) half a mile east of Jamaica village on which Mr. Seabury Rector of the church now lives. It contains 28 acres of good land, a good dwelling house (one end new), a genteel building, a dry cellar under the whole house, a well of good water, new barn, hovel and smokehouse. There is a fine orchard that makes 50 barrels of cider; also a screw-press and cider-mill of a new invention that grinds 50 bushels of apples in an hour. Also 14 acres of woodland 2 miles from the farm, and 8 acres of salt meadow that cuts 20 loads of salt hay.

Apply to the above said Samuel Seabury, Jr., who will give a good title."

STATE OF THE CHURCH.

Mr. Seabury still complains (1764) of the backwardness of his parishioners in complying with the christian sacraments, owing to the influence of quakerism and infidelity. Mr. Whitefield has again visited the Island whose tenets and methods of preaching have been adopted by many Dissenting Teachers, and strolling preachers who misrepresent the church of England as papists and teaching her members to expect salvation on account of their own works and deservings; but no church people have been led away, and many have become more serious and devout. He has baptized within a year 11 adults, 40 white, 25 black children. He has 28 communicants. A friendly disposition has subsisted between Dissenters and church people ever since he has been here. 1765, he observes his people are more friendly to each other and promise to be more punctual in paying him the allowance for house-rent, which if they perform his situation will be as good as he has a right to expect. From Michaelmas 1764 to Michaelmas 1765 he has baptized 26 white and 7 black children.

SEABURY LEAVES.

On Dec. 3, 1766, Mr. Seabury with consent of the Ven. Society * to his request was instituted rector of St. Peter's Church, Westchester. He writes July 25, 1767, that "before I left Jamaica I baptized there 4 adults and 3 infants. I have made two visits there since and baptized 1 adult, 2 white children and 3 black ones, and I must do the people at Newtown the justice to say that since my removal they sent me £20 currency. There are here no burial fees, but the wealthy sometimes give me a linen scarf, marriage fees are from one to four spanish dollars.

NOTE*—The Ven. Society was incorporated June 16, 1701.

REV. JOSHUA BLOOMER,

Rector, 1769 to 1790, was born in Westchester, and in 1759 was captain in the Provincial forces and afterwards a merchant in N. Y. He failed in business but in after years when he acquired money he devoted it to the payment of his debts. He was an unselfish man. Having once married a couple where a generous fee might well have been expected, an inquisitive person asked him next day the amount of his fee. "O I had forgotten all about it," he replied. "It must be in my other pocket." On searching for it 2 or 3 guineas were found wrapped up in paper. He died Wed. June 3, 1790, at the age of 55, "universally regretted," and was buried in the chancel. The church owed him a balance of £14 6. 9, at his death. He had been recommended to the Ven. Society by the Rev. Dr. Johnson and several other clergymen as a studious young man of a very fair character, and desirous to enter the ministry. He was accordingly ordained by the Bishop of London, and appointed Missionary with a grant of £30 yearly to the Parish of Jamaica, Flushing and Newtown at the earnest request of the people signified to the Society by the church wardens of those towns.

STATE OF THE CHURCH.

Mr. Bloomer writes that he came passenger in the Britannia to N. Y., and so to Jamaica safely in May, 1769, and was kindly received by the people. He finds the church at Jamaica a neat well finished building, but those at Newtown and Flushing small. He has 39 communicants who by their constant attendance and unblemished life are an honor to religion. In 1771 he again writes that he has been happy from the day of his arrival in the affections of his people expressed by every mark of kindness and respect which renders him the more able to engage their minds to religion, the good effect of which is already conspicuous in their constant attendance on public worship, and in the prevailing sense of a holy life. He officiates in course on Sundays at his 3 churches, and expounds the scriptures in the week to his people who have a great desire for instruction. He cultivates peace and love with people of other persuasions in the neighborhood.

NOTE.*—1704 June 16, arrived in N. Y., the Rev. Mr. Urquhart, minister of Jamaica. He came from England in the Faulkland, man of war, in consequence of the sea being infested with French and Spanish privateers.

NOTE.*—1722 June 13, Mr. Poyer inducted Mr. Jenney as Rector of Rye.

RECORDS.

Mr. Bloomer's records of marriages begin July 6, 1769; but the records of baptisms before June 1, 1780 are lost. Thus no records of Urquhart, Colgan or Seabury can now be found. Mr. Bloomer's original record-book bound in vellum disappeared after Parson Johnson's death, though fortunately he had copied it into a book of his own. So Grace Church is unfortunate in the loss of many of her old records.

STATE OF THE CHURCH.

Mr. Bloomer says (Feb. 15, 1770) I preach at the three churches alternately and generally to crowded assemblies, who behave with decorum. The churches are neat and well finished. Tho' I enjoy the love and esteem of my hearers, I have a troublesome lawsuit against the Parish for £60 yearly salary of which I have not received a farthing for years.

CHURCH WARDENS SUED.

Mr. Bloomer was inducted, Tuesday, May 23, 1769, but the wardens refused to pay his salary. He had to institute a suit in Chancery against Hendrickson & Edsall. It was long depending and not till April 1774 did Gov. Tryon the Chancellor decide in Bloomer's favor, each party to pay their own costs. To alleviate the misfortune of the losing party, Mrs. Tryon before her departure for London, kindly made them a present of the costs amounting to £80. Noble woman!

NOTE.*—Hinchman as church warden before the Rev. War had invested £100 of the church money which was repaid to him in 1776, in Continental bills; but in 1780 the British Police Court, at Jamaica, obliged him to pay over this money with interest (£120) in coin to Mr. Bloomer. On petition of his widow Joanna to the Legislature in 1790 the money was refunded.

CHANCELLOR'S DECREE.

"I decree that the defendants shall on or before the 4th day of June next, at the door of the Parish church of Jamaica, between the hours of 10 and 12 in the forenoon pay Mr. Bloomer his salary from the time of his Induction May 23, 1769 to the commencement of his suit, in this Court, out of any moneys that may have accrued under the Ministry Act, and have been received by the defendants as church-wardens prior to the filing of the bill, but without any interest. And I recommend the Parish of Jamaica to pay all arrears of salary to the Rev. Mr. Bloomer that are due him since filing the bill as any delay or further dispute would justly subject them to payment of costs."

REVOLUTIONARY WAR.

Mr. Bloomer writes that the principal members of his congregation who refused to join the measures of the Congress in 1775-6, had their houses plundered, their persons seized, some put in prison, others sent under guard to Conn. "I administered the Sacrament at Newtown, where I had but 4 or 5 male communicants, the rest being driven off or carried away prisoners. I was forbidden to read the Prayers for the King and Royal family. On consulting my wardens and vestry (rather than omit any portion of the liturgy) we shut up our church for 5 weeks; but on the arrival of the King's troop services were resumed and in 1777, I had 66 communicants." In 1780 Rev. John Sayre assisted him. At the close of the war his pay from the Ven. Society ceased.

CHURCH GLEBE.

In 1778, £800 was raised by lottery to lay out for a glebe; and the farm of W. Creed a mile west of the village was purchased, "70 acres of arable land, which will always be a considerable support for the Missionary. The buildings need improvement to make the place comfortable and convenient." The glebe did not suit as well as was expected and was sold." Money toward purchasing a globe had been previously raised by lottery as appears by the following advertisement:

JAMAICA PARISH CHURCH
Lottery, 5th and Last Class.

Scheme, viz:

1	prize of	$300	is	$300
1	do	200	"	200
1	do	100	"	100
4	do	50	"	200
10	do	20	"	200
30	do	10	"	300
50	do	8	"	400
575	do	4	"	2300

672	Prizes.	$4000
1328	Blanks.	

2000 tickets at $2 each are $4000 equal to £1600. At 15 per cent. deduction £240. Not two blanks to a prize.

☞ The managers of the Jamaica Parish Glebe Lottery take this opportunity to return their sincere thanks to their friends for the assistance they have given, in befriending the 4 classes of the GLEBE LOTTERY, which enabled them to finish the classes much sooner than they had reason to expect,—but as the dispatch occasioned a number of the tickets to remain on hand to the church, which having proved unfortunate, they flatter themselves of this last indulgence of their friends in giving their assistance to the above scheme.

New York, Feb 25, 1772.

SUBSCRIPTIONS

for painting and shingling the church, Aug. and Sept. 1786:

	£	s.		£	s
Edward Bardin,	2		Dan. Kissam		
Thos. Betts,		15	(at the Fly)	2	
Sam. Brownjohn,	3		Christopher Smith	5	
Joshua Bloomer,	2		Margaret Smith	2	
Thos. Colgan			Abm. Skinner(law)	2	10
(not paid)	1		John Tromp,		5

Dr. John Charlton	3	Robt. Troupe,	3 5
Jas. Depeyster,	3	Wm. Waters,	9
Sam. Eldert.		16 John I. Waters,	9
Wm. Edgar,	2	Thos. Welling,	1
Samson Fleming,	2	Sam. Welling,	1

NOTE*—1786, Feb. 9. "For sale, the farm belonging to the Episcopal church in Jamaica, pleasantly situated a mile west of the village. It contains 70 acres (6 of which is woodland) good for pasture or tillage. It has a house, barn and young orchard with a variety of other fruit. Inquire of Christopher Smith, Jamaica; Dan. Kissam, Flushing Fly, or Rev. Mr. Bloomer, Newtown." In 1788, Mr. Bloomer spent £79.19.9. in repairs on the glebe. In 1788, Jacob Bedell served as clerk at £5 a year. In 1792, the vestry vo c that his character shall be looked after.

Antiquities of Grace Church, No. 3.

WM. HAMMELL, Rector, 1790 to 1795, was called Aug. 1, 1790, at a salary of £40 per year from Jamaica and £25 or £30 in lieu of the glebe. Newtown paid £40, and Flushing £35.

MARRIED

in N. Y., Oct. 22, 1791, Rev. Wm. Hammell of Jamaica to Mrs. Catharine Piercy widow of Capt. Piercy of the British Navy.

In 1791, candles for the lecture cost 7s. 6d. Dec. 30, 1793, a subscription was started to buy a horse, saddle and bridle for Mr. Hammell. Newtown paid £5 18; Flushing £10, and Jamaica £17 8. The horse was bought of Wm. Golder for £34.

In 1792, the glebe was sold to John Van Liew for £603 10 and the money lent on bond to Elias Hicks £225; to John B. Hicks £290; to Christ'r Smith £165.

Mr. Hammell's eyesight became so weak that he could not well see to read prayers in public service, so he resigned Aug. 1, 1795; but his people paid his salary up to Nov. and added a gift of $100.

DIED

on the afternoon of Feb. 17, 1840, after a short illness, in the 78th year of his age, Rev. W. Hammell of the Episcopal Church. The friends and acquaintances and those of his son Wm. H. Hammell are respectfully invited to attend his funeral to-morrow afternoon, 19th inst., at 4 o'clock, from No. 31 Downing st., N. Y.

COMMUNICANTS 1791-3.

Mrs. Ann Betts. Jas. and Milla Mack.
James, Sarah, Ann, and Isaac and Mary Petit.
Ann B. Depeyster. Aaron Van Nostrand.
John and Mary Dodley. Jacob Van Peit.
John and Deborah Dunn Aletta Warne.
Catharin Hammell. Christopher and Mary
Jas. and Sarah Morrell. Smith.

CHARLES SEABURY,

son of the Bishop was called Jan. 15, 17 5 and left Mar. 2d.

Elijah D. Rattoone

was called May 12, 1797, at a salary of £250 per year, from Jamaica, and the interest of £900 which the church had in bonds from the sale of the glebe. He resigned June 4, 1802, and went to S. Paul's church, Baltimore. He had married in 1791, the daughter of Rev. Dr. Beach of N. Y. His residence was the place since Miller's, and is thus described April 23, 1802:

For Sale.

"A country seat in Flushing, on the road from Jamaica, containing 110 acres, being land bought by Benj. Cock of Thos. Wil... at 1793. On it is a new house 44 by 30 feet, with a kitchen and bedroom for servants in the basement, and 6 bedrooms on the 2d story. It is on a lofty eminence with a view of Newtown, Flushing and its bay, the Sound, Westchester and the Jersey shore. The ground slopes from the house which overlooks the farm, and is approached by avenues of butternut and poplar trees. It has pear and cherry trees and 1200 peach trees transplanted from Prince's nursery. Enquire of Rev. Dr. Beach, N. Y., or Rev. Mr. Rattoone on the premises.'

In 1797 Jas. Mackerel bought the place of Eliphalet Wickes for a church glebe at a cost of £300.

In 1797 the glebe of Grace Church was purchased by Jas. Depeyster, and in 1803 the vestry decided that Mrs. Depeyster must take nothing that is fast from the glebe.

In 1798 John V. Nostrand and Elizabeth Johnson rented the glebe, and in 1799 V. Nostrand and Mr. Price.

In 1799 a stove was got for the church.

In 1800 the small house and lot produced a yearly rent of £24.

In 1801 Miss Wolfendale and her pupils are allowed the use of a square pew.

In 1815, Oct. 20, the glebe was sold to Dr. N. Shelton for $1250.

Feb. 22d, 1800, was commemorated in honor of the virtues and talents of George Washington at Jamaica, when Mr. Rattoone said prayers, Mr. Elsenbrook delivered the oration, and two odes composed by Mr. Faitoute were sung. The procession was formed in front of the Episcopal Church and marched to the old stone church, the pulpit, desk and gallery of which were shrouded in black.

The Church Funds

on examination in 1794 proved to be in an unsatisfactory condition. Phillip Van Cortland's bond for ... in 1772 and 14 years interest due on it; Henry Dawson's bond for ... 7. 7, had 15 years interest due, and Benj. Carpenter's bond of £23 5. 7. and 19 years' interest due.

CALVIN WHITE

was inducted July 21, 1803. The vestry and clergy dined at Mrs. Waters'. His salary was $500 and the use of the glebe, which John V. Nostrand the tenant was requested to give up to him Dec. 10, 1802. There seemed to be a mutual misunderstanding between him and the vestry. The vestry were displeased at his alleged want of candor. He left Aug. 17, 1804. Mr. White left the Presbyterian church and passed thro' the Episcopal on his way to Rome. He was, it is said, an accomplished scholar and thorough master of Hebrew. He was widely known and loved. His life was pure, heart kind and manners courteous. He died at Derby, Conn., in 1853, aged 90. Ri. Grant White the literateur is his grandson.

MARRIED

Oct. 23, 1792, by the Rev. Dr. McWhorter, the Rev. Calvin White, minister of Hanover, N. J., to Miss Phebe Camp of Newark.

"Happy the youth that finds the bride
Whose birth is to his own allied,
The sweetest joy of life." *Hodls.*

GEORGE STREBECK,

who had served 6 months at North Salem, was called for 6 months from May 1, 1805. There is no record of his services here as Christopher Smith then died. Mr. Strebeck had been a Lutheran. He was deposed for intemperance when rector of St. Stephen's church, N. Y. After that he kept school and his sun went down in a cloud. Rev. S. R. Johnson once when travelling out West stopped for the night at a tavern and saw a man in seedy clothing sitting in the barroom. Toward bedtime the landlord said: "Strebeck it's time now for you to go home."

ANDREW FOWLER

was called for 6 months, Ap. 8th, 1806. He was born at Rye in 1760, kept school there and read prayers for 6 months at the close of the Revolutionary war. He was ordained priest 1790 and for 2 years had charge of the churches of Setauket, Huntington and Oyster Bay. Thence he went to Courtland. He died respected and beloved at Charleston, Dec. 9, 1850, aged 90.

JOHN IRELAND,
who had served at Westchester and Brooklyn, was called for 6 months from May 1, 1807. He died as chaplain in the Brooklyn navy yard, Mar. 25, 1822, aged 66. He was born in England, the son of a British Revolutionary officer. He was a scholar of polished manners and pleasing voice.

EDMUND S. BARRY,
a classical teacher in N. Y., of Irish birth, was called for a year for $500. The vestry also paid his stage expenses, and board from Sat. night till Monday morning.

TIMOTHY CLOWES
was called Ap. 23, 1809, at a salary of $700, and left Ap. 9, 1810, for S. Peter's, Albany. He was a graduate of Col. College, served S. Matthew's church, Jersey City, from Aug. 1, 1808, till he came to Jamaica. He boarded at widow Dunbar's and became engaged to her niece Mary. The engagement was subsequently broken off by mutual consent. The people would not let the matter drop thus, but took sides for and against their minister. Mr. Clowes having allowed some disparaging remarks to escape his lips, Miss Dunbar at the instigation of her friends brought suit against him in the Supreme Court, N. Y., Oct. 30, 1810, by her attorney, Martin S. Wilkins. The ablest counsel were employed on both sides and the jury rendered a verdict, May 4, 1812, of $1,000 damages and 6 cents costs.—*Eve. Post and Mer. Adv.*, Ap. 25, 1812.

Mr. Clowes was a large, raw-boned man, but beneath a rough exterior he had a cultivated mind. He published a volume of sermons and some mathematical works. Most of his life was spent in teaching. In 1830 he started a weekly paper called *The Schoolmaster*. He closed his chequered career at Hempstead, the place of his nativity, June 19, 1847, at the age of 60, having received the last consolations of the church

GILBERT H. SAYRES
was called May 1, 1810, at a salary of $750 per year. He was a graduate of Col. College 1808, studied for the ministry with Rev. Dr. Lyell of N. Y., and was ordained priest by Bishop Hobart in Zion Church, N. Y., Feb. 27, 1812. At his first coming he wore the conventional dress of that day. viz: breeches buckled at the knee, black stockings, and shoes. He retired from the charge May 1, 1830, on an allowance of $100 per year for five years. He died Ap. 27, 1867, aged 80, having received the degree of S. T.

D., in 1863.

He first occupied the house now Dr. Wood's but in 1812 the place of Smith Hicks was bought for him at a cost of £632. In 1820 the parsonage farm was sold to the Rector for $1400.

Mr. Sayres' parents were Friends. When a mere boy in N. Y., instead of going to meeting on First Days, he strayed off to other churches to hear eloquent speakers, and especially to Rutger's st. Presbyterian church where he was captivated with Dr. Milledoler. His views changed and the painful duty was laid on him of forsaking the belief of his parents. His mother laid his defection deeply to heart and was so strict and conscientious a Friend that she could never attend his public ministrations, though otherwise she had all a mother's affection for him.

After Mr. Sayres retired from the rectorship he let no opportunity of doing good or of giving good advice pass by unimproved. The poor and humble found in him a benefactor and counsellor. He was a great reader and his mind was well furnished with useful knowledge. Having enjoyed the society of statesmen, lawyers, and prominent men, he had a good store of interesting anecdotes that made his company desirable. He had overtasked his bodily and mental energies early in his ministry. Having for long years struggled against sundry ailments, by great care and prudence, his useful life was prolonged to an advanced age. He was emphatically the christian gentleman.

CHURCH REBUILT.

June 2d, 1820, the vestry resolved to repair and enlarge the old church; but at a meeting, Sept. 7th, a plan of a new church was submitted to their inspection and was approved. John Van Nostrand and John Thatford were the builders.

CONSECRATION.

1822, July 15, Monday morning the new and elegant church was consecrated by Bishop Hobart. His text was: "Take care how ye hear." The house was crowded to overflowing. Timothy Nostrand and L. E. A. Eigenbrodt wardens.

WM. L. JOHNSON

commenced here May 1, 1839, at $600 a year, and finding his own dwelling. He received the degree of D. D., from Allegheny College. He died Aug. 4, 1870, aged 70. Several of his sermons were published. He was a man of a cultivated mind and generous to excess, having never learned the art of hoarding up money.

CHRISTIAN COURTESY.

At a special meeting (1857, Nov. 23,) the vestry expressed their deep sympathy with the congregation of the Ref. Dutch church in the severe dispensation of being deprived of the use of their house of worship by fire, and tendered them the use of their church on Sunday afternoons, and direct that seats be provided for such of them as may wish to attend our regular services.

Signed, JER. VALENTINE, Clerk.

1859, May 8.—The vestry concluded to repair the church, and Aug. 26, it was reopened and a grand *Te Deum* performed.

1861.—About 3 o'clock on New Year's morning, a fire from the flue of the furnace was discovered. The newly repaired church was destroyed with most of its contents, organ, two tablets, communion table, etc. The bell was cast at Elizabethtown in 1768. The tombstones under and near the building were crumbled. Value $18,000, insured for $6,000.

1861, May 21.—The vestry contracted with Anders Peterson, mason, and Hendrick Brinckerhoff, carpenter, to build a Gothic edifice of Jersey bluestone, size 43 by 90 feet, the tower 12 feet square on S. W. corner to be 112 feet high. July 6th, the corner stone was laid by Bishop Potter. Among other things it contained a list of the officers of the church, viz:

Rev. Wm. L. Johnson, D. D., Rector.
Hendrick Brinckerhoff,
John A. King.   Wardens.

Vestrymen.

Wm. J. Cogswell.	Daniel Smith.
Jeremiah Valentine.	Samuel T. Woodley.
Dr. G. H. Kissam.	James J. Brenton.
John L. Denton.	John Demott Bergen.

On Sunday, Sep. 21, 1862, the new church was opened for Divine service. The Rector officiated, assisted by Rev. S. J. Corneille. The organ was the gift of Gov. King, the bishop's chair and books for the reading desk the gift of his family.

EXCHANGE OF CHRISTIAN COURTESY.

At a meeting of the vestry, Oct. 8, 1862, the following letter was drawn up:

To the Consistory of the Ref. Dutch Church, Jamaica.

Gentlemen:—Whereas with great liberality and true christian spirit you gave the use of your Consistory Room to the congregation of Grace Church (on the destruction of its edifice by fire) for the purpose of Divine worship; therefore, Resolved that our best thanks are hereby tendered you for the very acceptable and comfortable accommodations furnished us; and the congregation will ever hold in grateful remembrance this act of liberality and consideration.

Signed.   JER. VALENTINE,
Clerk of the Vestry.

BELL.

The amalgam bell was rejected and a new one from Meneely hung Oct. 6, 1862. It weighed over 1200 lbs.

CONSECRATION.

On Thursday, Jan. 8, 1863, Bishop Potter consecrated the church in presence of 20 clergymen. The instrument of donation and endowment was presented to the Bishop by John A. King. The Bishop gave the sentence of consecration to the Rector who read it to the congregation and gave it back to the Bishop who laid it on the communion table. Th Bishop preached a sermon to a large audience.

S. J. CORNIELLE

left for All Saints' church, N. Y., May 16, 1863. Services were held in the church every Friday evening during Lent.

AUGUSTUS W. CORNELL

was called Jan. 1864, as Rector's assistant, and ordained priest by Bishop Potter Ap. 1.

THOS. COOK

was called 1866, May 10, as assistant to the Rector who was now infirm.

G. WILLIAMSON SMITH

officiated here for the first time Nov. 26, 1871 and was called Feb. 6, 1872.

Antiquities of Grace Church. No. 9.
JAMAICA.

The first Episcopal Church on L. I., was at Jamaica; the second one at Hempstead, as appears by the following extracts from authentic documents.

The Ven. Society printed no reports before 1704; but Rev. Geo. Keith says: "I arrived at Boston, June 11, 1702, with Rev. Patrick Gordon who died six weeks after at Jamaica of a violent fever then frequent at N. Y., where he first had it as is thought." The report of Ven. Society (1704) says: "Granted Patrick Gordon, Rector of Queens county, £50 per annum, since deceased." "Granted to Wm. Urquhart at Jamaica £50 per annum."

☞"A minister is wanted for Hempstead who will be allowed £60 there per annum."

The Rev. Wm. Urquhart arrived in N. Y., June 16th and on July 4th took possession of the Parsonage and was inducted in Aug. 1704. But before his arrival the Gov'r. had already granted Rev. James Honeyman admission to the ministerial function in Jamaica where he was serving in April 1704 and hoped by God's blessing to be of considerable service to the church. He had left his station in the navy by command of the Ven. Society on purpose to serve at Jamaica, where he says "We have a church, but not those necessaries that are requisite to the daily discharge of our office, namely, neither Bible nor Prayer Book, no cloths for pulpit or altar." * In a letter of the N. Y. Clergy to the Ven. Society they say: "in 1702, Rev. Patrick Gordon came from England to the church at Jamaica, who before he could be inducted was snatched away by death from those people to their unspeakable loss; and upwards of 50 persons petitioned Gov'r. Cornbury that he would give such directions to Rev. Mr. Vesey that they might have constant lectures amongst them till that loss should be made up."

NOTE—*On the arrival of Mr. Urquhart, Mr. Honeyman was sent to Newport where he died after over 40 years service.

Mr. Gordon was buried by Mr. Vesey, Tuesday July 28, under the communion table in the old stone church and when it was taken down his remains and those of Mr. Urquhart were translated to the village cemetery. Another account says: "Patrick Gordon went from N. Y., with design to preach in his Parish (at the invitation of some of the best men in it) but took sick the day before he designed to preach, and so continued till his death about eight days after. God took him away just as he was about entering upon his charge."

Administration was granted on his estate (Dec. 5, 1702) to Lewis Morris, Esq., who, with Samuel Clowes and Caleb Heathcote took great interest in the success of the Jamaica Church.

LORD CORNBURY,

the Gov. of N. Y. has been blamed for meddling with the church affairs of Queens County; but he seems to have done little more (except disregarding the forms of law) than carry out the *instructions* given him by his superiors, who wished the church of England to be established here.* We give four extracts:

60.—"You shall take care that God be duly and devoutly served throughout your government, that the Book of Common Prayer be read each Sunday and Holiday and that the sacraments be administered according to the rites of the church of England; that the churches be orderly and well kept and more built as the Colony improves.

Besides the maintenance to each Minister of an Orthodox church a house shall be built for him at the common charge and land assigned for a glebe and the exercise of his industry.

61.—You shall prefer no minister to a benefice without he has a certificate from the Bishop of London of his being conformable to the doctrine and discipline of the church of England and of a good life and conversation.

62.—You shall give order that every Orthodox minister be one of the Vestry and that there be no meeting without him except he be sick or omit to come.

63.—You shall enquire if there be any Minister who preaches and administers the sacrament in any Orthodox church or chapel without being in due orders; and you are to give account thereof to the Bishop of London."

MAXIMS OF ENGLISH LAW.

"All meeting houses raised by public tax become vested in the ministry established by law and so of all lands and glebes set aside by public Town Meetings.

Every church of common right is entitled to a house and glebe; and they belong to the Rector *ex-officio*."

NOTE.—* The former Governors had encouraged equality among the sects; but Cornbury strove to introduce the English Statutes of Uniformity, in obedience to the instructions he had received (Dec. 5, 1702) from Queen Anne.

After the Presbyterians were deprived of their meeting house, they renewed their complaint to each successive Governor. We give one that has never before been printed:

"The Memorial of Nathaniel Denton, Thos. Waters, and John Everett to Gov. Lovelace:

Jamaica was bought in 1656 from the Indians by our ancestors subjects of the realm of England, Protestants (Dissenters in manner of worship from the forms used in the church of England) who settled and improved the lands and called Ministers of their own profession to officiate amongst them till 1703.

In 1676 the Townsmen set apart divers lands for the better support of such ministers; and in 1693 bought a house and other conveniences for their accommodation.

About 1699 the major part of the freeholders built a meeting house for the worship of God in their own way, and peaceably used it till 1703-4, when without trial or process at law they were with force turned out, and are still deprived of the house, lands and other conveniences of said meeting house.

† All which, in behalf of the people of Jamaica, we submit to your Lordship's consideration and pray such relief as consists with equity and justice."

The Governor sent this Memorial to Rev. Wm. Urquhart the incumbent and Rector, who (April 4, 1709) thus replied:

"Of what sect in religion the purchasers of Jamaica were I know not; but am certain that the surviving Patentees were neither Presbyterians nor Independents. In 1676 they set apart land for a Parsonage to continue at the disposal of the Town to a "Minister" which [word] being not expressly mentioned [or defined] cannot mean "Dissenters," much less any particular sect of them; but by intendment of law designs an *Orthodox* Minister of the established church of the realm of England, which [opinion] is favored by many adjudged cases on the Statute of Charitable Uses. On Sep. 29, 1693 [the Rev. John] Prudden sold back to the Town the Parsonage-house and home-lot (which they before had given him,) "to have and to hold as a Parsonage for the use of *the Ministry* for ever," which grant in all legal construction must be construed in favor of the *Established Church*. In 1698 by Act of Assembly a Church was built in the middle of the street. It is called *a Church by them*, and a very great many of the principal builders have always declared that they intended it for *a Church of England*. Besides, the very words of the Act, viz: "that there shall be called, *inducted* and established a good sufficient Protestant minister," can mean no other. For it was never known that any sect of Dissenters ever called their place of public worship "a church," or that they elected "Church Wardens" and "Vestrymen," or that their ministers received "Induction," as are the words of that Act of Assembly.

They complain of being "turned out," etc. It is true that when there was no Orthodox minister, a Presbyterian or Independent minister has had the possession of the church, house and lands (which was the case of Hempstead also, but all were willingly surrendered when demanded by Mr. Thomas); but that whenever a Church of England minister came, he always took possession of the church, which was in effect the possession of the whole. Besides, Mr. Hubbard was not "forcibly turned out" but on Lord Cornbury's order he quietly left; and they have since erected themselves a meeting house at their own charge.

Wherefore I heartily pray your Excellency as a good father and patron of the church will discourage these Memorialists as the disturbers of her peace."

The Governor requested the memoralists to draw up their objections to Mr. Urquhart's letter but he died before the case could be argued before him; and so nothing came of it. Mr. Urquhart also died about the first of September, and the Lieut. Gov. put the things belonging to the church in custody of Samuel Clowes, a true lover of the church, which was, he says, a great detriment to his secular affairs amongst the Dissenters his inveterate neighbors.

HEMPSTEAD CHURCH.

From the preceding quotations from cotemporary records it appears that Jamaica had three Episcopal ministers settled before Hempstead had one.

This statement is illustrated and confirmed by several authors:

(1). The Rev. Geo. Keith, an itinerant missionary of the Ven. Society, says: "On Sunday, Sep. 27, 1702, I preached at Hempstead where was such a multitude that the church [Presbyterian] could not contain them. Many stood without at the doors and windows to hear, who were generally well affected, and greatly desired a Church of England minister to be settled among them."

(2). Rev. John Bartow of W, C. says (May 24, 1704): "Hempstead has long expected a Missionary from the Ven. Society, and I hope they will soon be answered."

(3). Rev. Mr. Pritchard of Rye writes (Nov. 1, 1705) that "the Ven. Society would do well to send Mr. Stuart to Hempstead, where they stand very much in need of a minister, and complain very much for [want of] a Churchman, it being the best place in the Province of N. Y., and best affected for the church. I design to preach there (D. V.) frequently in order to continue them in a good opinion of our Church till a minister comes. Mr. Vesey * and the people of Hempstead have been very pressing on me to remove there, saying Lord Cornbury would willingly consent thereto."

Some one may say: "Well, if the Hempstead church is not older than that of Jamaica, what is the date of its establishment?" We let Mr. Thomas reply to this question in the very words that he himself wrote in the Register Book, July 13, 1707:

"I, John Thomas E. Coll. Jesu, Oxon. was inducted Rector of Hempstead, Dec. 27, 1704."

Mr. Thomas' name appears for the first time in the Ven. Society's Report of Feb. 16, 1705, when a grant of £50 had been made to him. Mr. Thomas writes to the Ven. Society (Mar. 1, 1705) that "the people of Hempstead are better disposed to peace and civility than they are at Jamaica, yet My Lord Cornbury's countenance (next to the Providence of Heaven) is my chiefest safety. I have scarce a man in the Parish truly steady and real to the interest and promotion of the church any further than they aim at the favor or dread the displeasure of his Lordship. At the first communion I could persuade but three to receive."

Caleb Heathcote writes (Nov. 9, 1705) that "Mr. Thomas has better assistants than Mr. Urquhart of Jamaica; the leading men of Hempstead not being disgusted, are helpful in the work, and having no other Sectaries to oppose him by their meetings, but the Quakers, he makes very considerable progress."

Queen Anne (1706) gave to Jamaica, Hempstead and three other churches each, a large Bible, Common Prayer, Homilies, cloths for pulpit and communion table, a silver chalice and paten.

NOTE.—* It was natural for Mr. Vesey to take interest in the growth of the church of Hempstead for when he labored there as an Independent or Congregational preacher he was called by the Dissenting Vestry, to Trinity Church, N. Y., in a seeming but compulsory compliance with law, they knowing him to be not qualified for the charge; but Mr. Vesey turned the tables on them, for as soon as he accepted and secured the call he changed his views, became a convert to Episcopacy, crossed the ocean and having received imposition of hands, and a certificate of his conformity from the Bishop of London, he returned to his cure and was inducted Rector of the parish to the great mortification of the baffled Vestry who were thus caught in their own trap.

www.ingramcontent.com/pod-product-compliance
Lightning Source LLC
Chambersburg PA
CBHW030332170426
43202CB00010B/1098